Neurology for Psychiatrists

To our wives,
Simrit, Survjeet and Denise respectively

Neurology for Psychiatrists

Gin S Malhi BSc (Hons), MRCPsych
Clinical Lecturer
Social Genetic and Developmental Research Centre
Institute of Psychiatry
London
UK

Manjit S Matharu BSc (Hons), MRCP
Clinical Research Fellow
Institute of Neurology
Queen's Square
London
UK

Anthony S Hale PhD, FRCPsych
Professor of Psychiatry
Kent Institute of Medicine and Health Sciences
University of Kent at Canterbury
UK

Wyeth

Presented with the compliments of Wyeth Laboratories

MARTIN DUNITZ

The views expressed in this publication are those of the author and not necessarily those of Wyeth Laboratories.

© Martin Dunitz Ltd 2000

First published in the United Kingdom in 2000 by
Martin Dunitz Ltd
The Livery House
7–9 Pratt Street
London NW1 0AE

Tel: +44-(0)20-7482-2202
Fax: +44-(0)20-7267-0159
E-mail: info@mdunitz.globalnet.co.uk
Website: http://www.dunitz.co.uk

A CIP catalogue record for this book is available from the British Library

ISBN 1-85317-933-7

Composition by Wearset, Boldon, Tyne and Wear
Printed and bound in Spain by Grafos, S.A.

Z782860

Contents

Foreword

Prior to the establishment of the Royal College of Psychiatrists in 1971, aspiring psychiatric trainees were usually advised to spend time in general medicine and neurology before joining their chosen speciality. Some trainees even obtained the MRCP qualification before starting psychiatry. Indeed, before the introduction of the MRCPsych examination, the only postgraduate qualification available in psychiatry was the 'Diploma of Psychological Medicine' or 'DPM'. These courses were offered by a few universities in the UK and Ireland, and usually included a clinical examination in neurology. Thus there was a clear understanding that postgraduate training in neurology was essential for the practice of psychiatry.

The development of psychiatry as a major independent speciality has led to its separation from general medicine and neurology in particular. Only in the realms of liaison psychiatry or concentrated in specialized centres such as The Institute of Neurology, Queen Square in London do the links remain. Expertise in neurology is no longer required for the trainee psychiatrist and the subject is not examined in the MRCPsych. It is understandable that the rapidly expanding knowledge base in psychiatry has meant that subjects have had to be dropped from the examination syllabus. Nonetheless, removing the requirement for neurology training represents a considerable loss of clinical expertise for more recently qualified psychiatric trainees.

The authors of *Neurology for Psychiatry* have clearly re-affirmed the importance of the speciality for psychiatric practice. They have produced a concise, easily read *vade mecum* of the aspects of neurology most salient to the assessment of those with mental illness. The book includes a detailed account of history taking, physical examination and investigations in neurology. After these basic principles, the authors have covered those topics of most relevance to psychiatry such as headaches, movement disorders, epilepsy and disorders of sleep and sexual function. The last chapter considers the relationship between neurological disorders and depression and includes discussions of drug side effects and interactions.

As one of a diminishing band of psychiatrists who has a 'DPM', I can readily acknowledge the importance of clinical neurology and its relevance to psychiatry. Although no longer as skilled in undertaking a full neurological examination as I was as a house officer, reading this book quickly reminded me of a previously acquired expertise. I am delighted to recommend *Neurology for Psychiatrists*. It is essential reading for psychiatric trainees who have not had any postgraduate experience in neurology, and will be most useful to those who wish to refresh their memory.

Anne E Farmer
Professor of Nosology
Social Genetic and Developmental Research
Centre
Institute of Psychiatry
London

Preface

Many psychiatrists receive little in the way of formal neurological training and yet the majority would agree that some understanding of neurology is essential in most, if not all, fields of psychiatry. Over the past few decades psychiatry has rapidly expanded and perhaps because of this some subjects such as neurology receive less attention than they should. It is with these reasons in mind that we have written this book for trainee psychiatrists and established clinicians alike. It was never our intention to write a comprehensive textbook of neurology as this would clearly defeat its purpose and so the book concentrates on history taking and examination and deals with areas of particular interest and relevance to psychiatrists such as headaches, sleep and sexual dysfunction. Movement disorders and epilepsy are also discussed in detail but there are obvious and deliberate omissions such as dementias, stroke and the effects of substance misuse. However, it was felt that these topics already receive sufficient attention as they are managed by specialists within psychiatry and, furthermore, including these topics would inevitably have compromised the extent to which other topics could be discussed. This book will be of natural interest to liaison psychiatrists and neuropsychiatrists but it is hoped that it will be read by all psychiatrists at every level and be of particular use to trainees and those embarking on a career in psychiatry.

GSM
MSM
ASH

Taking a neurological history

1

Neurological diagnosis relies on the fundamental skills of history taking and physical examination. The central theme in taking a neurological history is to determine the anatomical site of a lesion and its underlying pathology. A detailed and accurate history allows the clinician to tailor the neurological examination so that specific aspects of the neurological system can be targeted. Both history taking and physical examination require considerable skill, and the best way to master these

Table 1.1
Components of a neurological history.

> History of the presenting complaint
> Family history
> Personal history
>   childhood and adolescence
>   psychosexual history
>   occupational history
>   social history
>   premorbid personality
> Past medical, surgical and psychiatric history
> Current medication
> History of substance misuse

skills is practice. From the history alone the clinician is likely to be able to develop several probable hypotheses. The physical examination is then used to confirm or refute these hypotheses and arrive at a list of differential diagnoses. These are then incorporated into a formulation that includes any necessary investigations and outlines the clinical management of the patient's problems.

History

A neurological history is taken in much the same manner as in other fields of medicine (*Table 1.1*). However, it is important that a systematic review of neurological symptoms is included, and within this there should be enquiry about each of the following.

• Pain
Head, facial, neck, back and limb pain.
(Note that pain is the most common reason for seeking medical attention. It is in itself a clinical entity.)

• Changes in the level of consciousness
Blackouts, faints, fits and sleep disturbance.
(Note that patients often forget such events and may therefore need to be 'reminded'.)

• Cognitive functions
Memory, concentration, mood and language.
(Note that patients are often unaware of such

problems or may be reluctant to acknowledge them.)

• Cranial nerve symptoms
Visual loss and blurred or double vision.
Changes in hearing, balance, smell and taste.
Vertigo and dizziness.
Speech problems and difficulty in swallowing.

• Motor symptoms
Weakness, clumsiness or stiffness of limbs.
Gait disorder.
Involuntary movements or a lack of co-ordination.

• Sensory symptoms
Numbness, paraesthesia and hyperalgesia.

• Urogenital symptoms
Bladder, bowel and sexual dysfunction.

When inquiring about these symptoms it is important to consider the temporal features of each, since these aspects often hold vital clues for diagnosis:

(a) time of onset;
(b) progression;
(c) duration;
(d) recovery; and
(e) frequency.

For example, in a patient who develops hemiparesis, a rapid onset (over seconds or minutes) points to a possible vascular cause, but a gradual onset (over days or weeks) is more suggestive of a slow-growing mass such as a tumour. Similarly, the progress of symptoms can give an indication of their cause; for example, a relapsing–remitting course is characteristic of processes involving demyelination or inflammation.

An area of particular importance, in the neurological context, is the family history, since many neurological disorders have a genetic basis. When a hereditary disorder is suspected, a detailed family pedigree should be constructed. In order to do this, it is often useful to interview other members of the family as well as the patient, and perhaps even to examine them and to carry out the necessary investigations. Other than the obvious benefit of aiding diagnosis, the presence of a family history of a particular disorder is likely to alter the patient's perception of his or her own illness, and this needs to be borne in mind when discussing investigations, treatments and prognosis.

It is important to note that the consultation of relatives is not limited to taking a family history. Not surprisingly, patients with neurological disorders often have difficulty in providing a clear history. For example, patients with language impairment and patients who have experienced an alteration in their level of consciousness are likely to find it difficult to describe their symptoms accurately. A witness of the events, a relative or a friend is invaluable in such cases.

There are many aspects to taking a history, most of which can be learnt or remembered, but the key to good history taking is practice. With experience the history-taking process can be adapted to the specific needs of each patient and to the constraints of various clinical settings.

Neurological examination

2

A thorough history will usually provide a clear working hypothesis as to the likely cause of a patient's neurological symptoms. A neurological examination is used to test this hypothesis by confirming or refuting diagnostic possibilities in order to arrive at differential diagnoses and define the aetiology anatomically by determining the possible site of a lesion.

Psychiatrists, even less so than neurologists, seldom need to perform a full neurological examination, but familiarity with neurological signs and components of the examination will no doubt aid their understanding of neurological syndromes. The aim of this chapter is to provide psychiatrists with the information necessary for them to be able to perform essential neurological tests and to equip them with the clinical knowledge needed to interpret a neurologist's findings.

Examination

The principal objective of a neurological examination is localization. The examination involves demonstrating functional neuroanatomy and consists of several groups of procedures and tests. The format is often adapted to the

Table 2.1
The neurological examination.

> Mental state
>   orientation, memory and higher
>   intellectual functions
> Speech
>   phonation, articulation and
>   language
> Cranial nerves I–XII
> Motor system
>   tone, strength and abnormal
>   movements, co-ordination
> Reflexes
> Sensory system
>   pain, touch, vibration sense and
>   temperature
> Gait

problem in hand, and the detail necessary for each component of an examination is determined largely by the symptomatology. However, it is important that no part of the examination is omitted completely, since this may cause crucial signs to be overlooked.

Table 2.1 details the components of a complete neurological examination.

Functionally, the neurological examination is divided somewhat arbitrarily. However, it usually begins with an appraisal of the mental state, and this is logical since this tests the most fundamental functions of the brain,

which, if impaired, are likely to affect other components of the examination.

Language also warrants particular attention since it involves many regions of the brain and deficits are likely to make communication difficult.

The cranial nerves are usually tested next, either individually or in groups, and this can often be a lengthy process. However, it is time well spent since cranial nerve signs usually allow accurate localization.

In examining the motor system, greater attention should be paid to the pattern of any weakness as opposed to its extent or severity because this is more likely to indicate the origin of the weakness. There are three essential patterns:

(a)   weakness on one side of the body (hemiplegia) is indicative of contralateral brain damage;

(b)   weakness of both legs (paraparesis) suggests spinal cord damage; and

(c)   weakness limited to distal portions of limbs is a feature of damage to the peripheral nervous system rather than to the central nervous system.

This last distinction can also be made by testing the deep tendon reflexes, which are normally examined next. Pathological reflexes, such as frontal release signs, are also tested for at this stage.

The examination of the sensory system is

Table 2.2
The Glasgow coma scale.

	Patient's response	Score
Eye opening	Spontaneous	4
	To speech	3
	To pain	2
	None	1
Best verbal response	Oriented	5
	Confused	4
	Inappropriate words	3
	Incomprehensible sounds	2
	None	1
Best motor response	Obeying commands	6
	Localizing pain	5
	Withdrawing to pain	4
	Flexing to pain	3
	Extending to pain	2
	None	1

Each component is rated separately, and a total score of between 3 and 15 is ascribed. A patient with normal consciousness should score a total of 15.

less objective than other components of the examination and can consume a considerable length of time. It usually involves testing pain, touch, temperature, vibration and joint position sense.

Finally, cerebellar function is examined using a variety of tests, and the individual's gait is also assessed.

Mental state and higher intellectual functions

Consciousness

Consciousness is defined as 'an individual's sense of self and of the environment'.

Normal consciousness depends on sensory input to the brain. The reticular activating system maintains the cerebral cortex in an alert state.

The Glasgow coma scale (*Table 2.2*) is a quick, simple and reliable method for recording and monitoring a patient's level of consciousness.

Mental state

The mental state examination forms an essential part of both psychiatric and neurological practice. Examination of the mental state should be recorded as follows.

• Appearance and general behaviour
Assessment begins on meeting the patient and should be as thorough and comprehensive as possible. A note should be made of the context in which these observations are made.

• Talk
It is the form (e.g. spontaneous or fast) that is noted as opposed to content.

• Mood
The patient should be questioned in detail about his or her mood, and, if indicated, specific enquiry should made about guilt, self-esteem, suicidal ideation, hopelessness and tearfulness, along with a review of biological symptoms such as changes in appetite, weight and libido. The patient should also be questioned about symptoms of anxiety.

• Thought content
Questions should explore the presence of morbid thoughts and preoccupations and

specifically ask about obsessional ruminations and phobias.

• Abnormal beliefs and interpretations
The onset, content and degree of conviction with which abnormal beliefs are held about the patient's self, body or environment needs to be noted.

• Abnormal experiences
Abnormal experiences may also be in relation to the self, body or environment, and when present their content, source and timing and the reality with which they are experienced should be recorded.

• Cognitive state
This involves testing orientation, attention, concentration and memory and gauging the patient's intelligence from all the information available (see Mini-mental state examination, below).

• Insight
The patient's understanding of his or her illness and its difficulties and prognosis is assessed.

Mini-mental state examination

The mini-mental state examination (MMSE, *Table 2.3*) was developed at Johns Hopkins University, Baltimore, to be used in neurological patients; however, it is now also used in many other settings. It is good for

Table 2.3
*Mini-mental state examination. (From Folstein MF, Folstein SE, McHugh PR. Mini-mental state examination: a practical method for grading cognitive state of patients for the clinician. J Psychiatr Res 1975; **12**; 189–98.)*

Orientation
Score 1 point for each correct answer:
  What is the time, date, day, month and year? *(5 points)*
  What is the name of the country, town, district, hospital and ward? *(5 points)*

Registration
Name three objects. Ask the patient to repeat the names of the three objects, scoring 1 point for each correct answer. *(3 points)*

Repeat the above part of the test until the patient can repeat all three objects, so as to test recall later.

Attention and concentration
Serial sevens test:
  Ask the patient to subtract 7 from 100, and then 7 from the result. Repeat this a total of five times and score 1 point for each time a correct subtraction is performed. *(5 points)*

Alternatively, ask the patient to spell 'world' backwards and score 1 point for each correct letter (D L R O W).

Recall
Ask for the names of the three objects repeated in the registration test and score 1 point for each object that is recalled correctly. *(3 points)*

Language
Point to a pencil and a watch and ask the patient to name them. Score 1 point for each correct answer. *(2 points)*

Ask the patient to repeat, 'No ifs, ands or buts'. Score 1 point for correct repetition. *(1 point)*

Ask the patient to follow a three-stage command: 'Take the piece of paper in your right hand, fold the paper in half and place it on the floor'. Score 1 point for each part of the command that is carried out correctly. *(3 points)*

On a piece of paper write, 'CLOSE YOUR EYES', and ask the patient to obey what is written on the paper. Score 1 point. *(1 point)*

Ask the patient to write a sentence. Score 1 point if the sentence has a subject and a verb and makes sense. *(1 point)*

Ask the patient to copy two intersecting pentagons with equal sides. Score 1 point if this is correctly copied. *(1 point)*

TOTAL **30 points**

screening global cognitive dysfunction as opposed to focal cognitive dysfunction, and it is often used to screen for dementia (indicated by a score of less than 23). It has been widely validated in a variety of populations, but it is important to note that it is subject to variation with age, socioeconomic status and educational achievement; moreover, it is heavily weighted on verbal performance, which means that the performance of dysphasic patients is particularly poor.

In routine neurological practice, the assessments of mental state and cognitive function described above are usually sufficient. When specific deficits are suspected, more sophisticated examination (examples of which follow) may be necessary.

Cerebral functions

Lesions to either of the cerebral hemispheres can manifest themselves as hemisensory loss, hemiparesis, partial seizures or homonymous hemianopia. However, some deficits, such as agnosias and apraxias, are specific to either the dominant or non-dominant hemisphere, while other deficits, such as pseudobulbar palsy, are characteristic of bilateral cerebral involvement. *Table 2.4* summarizes the typical clinical features of cerebral lobe dysfunction.

Apraxia and agnosia are discussed here since they are considered to involve 'higher functions' and to involve the cerebral hemispheres. In practice, they are usually tested for after speech, motor and sensory examination because the tests rely on intact sensory and motor pathways.

Dyspraxia and apraxia

Dyspraxia is defined as 'difficulty in performing a complex motor task despite normal power, sensation, co-ordination, comprehension and co-operation'. Apraxia is the complete inability to perform such a task.

Functional neuroanatomy

Figure 2.1 shows the pathways involved in the formulation and performance of a skilled motor task (normal praxis). Requests for normal movements are received in the dominant posterior temporal lobe by Wernicke's area. From here they are transmitted through the dominant parietal lobe to the ipsilateral frontal lobe premotor area and thence to the contralateral motor strip of the non-dominant hemisphere via the corpus callosum. Apraxias are caused by lesions along this pathway.

Clinical examination

To demonstrate apraxia, first test the patient's ability to make gestures (symbolic acts) using the buccofacial musculature (lips, face and tongue) and the limbs. Then ask the patient to perform imagined and real actions. Examples are given in *Table 2.5.*

Table 2.4
Clinical syndromes associated with cerebral lobe dysfunction.

Lobe	Clinical features
Frontal	Contralateral hemiparesis and upper motor neurone facial weakness Expressive dysphasia (dominant lobe lesion) Behavioural change—alteration in personality, mood and initiative Loss of abstract thought Primitive reflexes Grasp reflex—flexion of fingers on stroking palm Sucking reflex—sucking response on stroking the lips Pouting reflex—pouting on tapping closed lips Gait apraxia Anosmia—loss of sense of smell
Parietal	Dominant parietal lobe Sensory impairment Impaired two-point discrimination Astereognosis Agraphaesthesia Receptive dysphasia Visual field defect—contralateral lower homonymous hemianopia Gerstmann's syndrome Right–left disorientation Finger agnosia—inability to recognize and identify fingers of the hand correctly Dyscalculia—impaired calculation Dyslexia—difficulty with reading Apraxia Non-dominant parietal lobe Visuospatial processing Constructional apraxia—difficulty with drawing or constructing objects Dressing apraxia—difficulty with dressing Contralateral sensory inattention Contralateral hemisensory loss
Temporal	Receptive dysphasia Auditory agnosia Visual field defect—contralateral upper homonymous quadrantanopia Memory impairment Emotional disturbances—aggression, rage and hypersexuality
Occipital	Visual field defect—contralateral homonymous hemianopia Visual agnosia

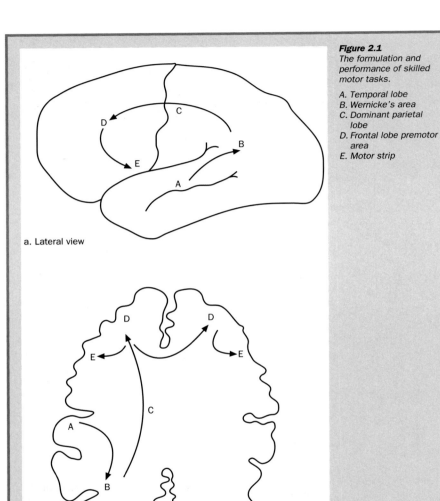

a. Lateral view

b. Horizontal section

Figure 2.1
The formulation and performance of skilled motor tasks.

A. Temporal lobe
B. Wernicke's area
C. Dominant parietal lobe
D. Frontal lobe premotor area
E. Motor strip

Table 2.5
Examination for apraxia.

	Symbolic act	**Imagined action**	**Real action**
Buccofacial	*Kiss the air*	*Suck on a straw*	*Drink water through a straw*
Limb	*Salute*	*Pretend to write*	*Write on a piece of paper*

The types of apraxia are:

(a) ideomotor apraxia, which is the inability to convert an idea into action. This is the most common type of apraxia and is usually caused by a dominant frontal or parietal lobe lesion;

(b) gait apraxia, which is a hallmark of normal-pressure hydrocephalus;

(c) ideational apraxia (conceptual apraxia), which is the inability to perform motor activities that require several sequential steps. It is often a manifestation of multi-infarct dementia or Alzheimer's disease; and

(d) constructional apraxia, which is the inability to draw shapes or to construct figures or geometrical patterns. It is usually associated with non-dominant parietal lobe lesions. (Note: constructional and dressing apraxias are strictly speaking visuo-spatial processing disorders).

Agnosia

Agnosia means non-recognition. It is the failure to appreciate the significance of sensory information in spite of intact sensory pathways and sensorium. Agnosias are indicative of lesions in sensory association areas and can occur in all sensory modalities.

The types of agnosia include:

(a) tactile agnosia (or astereognosis), which is the inability to recognize the form, texture and shape of objects using palpation alone in silence with the eyes closed. It arises from a lesion of the contralateral parietal lobe;

(b) visual agnosia, which is the inability to recognize a familiar object by inspection alone. It arises from a lesion of the dominant parieto-occipital lobe; and

(c) auditory agnosia, which is the inability to recognize a sound without seeing or touching the source of the sound. It arises from a lesion of the dominant temporal lobe.

Examination

The general principle when testing for agnosia is to observe the patient's appreciation of a sensory stimulus in the absence of cues from other sensory modalities.

Speech

Speech involves phonation, articulation and the production of language:

(a) phonation is the production of sound as air passes through the vocal cords;

(b) articulation is the manipulation of sound by the palate, tongue and lips as it passes through the upper airways to produce phonemes (single sounds); and

(c) the production of language involves the organization of phonemes into words and sentences by the speech centres in the dominant cerebral hemisphere (Broca's area and Wernicke's area).

Anatomy

The primary auditory cortex (Heschl's gyri) in each temporal lobe transmits language signals to Wernicke's area in the dominant temporal lobe, which is involved in the comprehension of spoken language. From here the signals pass via the arcuate fasciculus to reach Broca's area, in the dominant frontal lobe, which governs the

expression of speech. Neurones from Broca's area project to the motor area of the precentral gyrus. This is responsible for the control of speech musculature. Upper motor neurones project from the motor cortex to the nuclei of cranial nerves VII, IX, X and XII, and from these nuclei lower motor neurones supply the muscles involved in speech (*Fig. 2.2*). As with all movements, these neuronal pathways receive important modifying inputs from the basal ganglia and cerebellum.

Types of speech defects

The types of speech defects and their definitions are:

(a) dysphonia, which is a defect of speech volume;

(b) dysarthria, which is a defect of articulation with preserved language function; and

(c) dysphasia, which is a defect of language function in which there is abnormal comprehension or abnormal production of speech, or both.

Examination

It is important to note that 'normal' language varies considerably. Many people have their own unique style of talking and often falter or

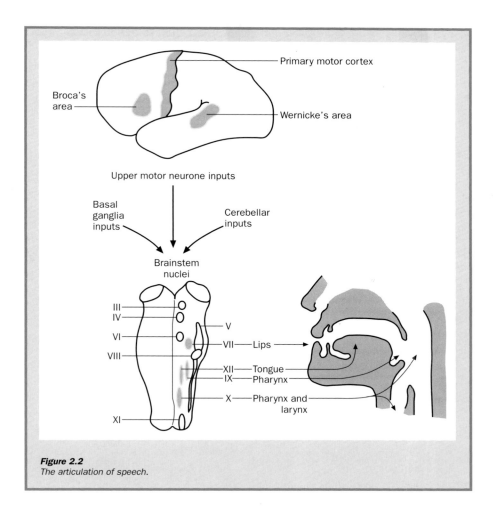

Figure 2.2
The articulation of speech.

change their pattern of speech because of social pressures or changes of mood. The steps in examining speech are as follows.

• Assess comprehension

Ask the patient simple questions (e.g. name, address and occupation). If the patient seems not to understand, then ask simpler questions with yes–no answers and give straightforward commands. If successful, ask increasingly complex questions and give complicated commands.

• Assess phonation

If the patient is able to speak then assess the volume of speech. If this is reduced, then ask the patient to cough and listen to the quality of the sound.

• Assess articulation

If the patient is able to speak then listen for any abnormalities of articulation. Ask the patient to repeat some difficult phrases (e.g. 'East Register Street is opposite West Register Street' or 'The British Constitution').

If articulation is abnormal in any way then assess the use of the letters 'p', 't' and 'k', which are facial, tongue and palatal sounds, respectively.

• Assess spontaneous speech

Assess fluency, which is the ability of the patient to produce phrases of normal length (five or more words) in spontaneous speech.

• Assess repetition

Ask the patient initially to repeat simple words and then increasingly complex sentences.

• Assess naming and word-finding ability

Ask the patient to name familiar objects and then go on to ask about the use of less familiar objects.

Interpretation of examination

Dysphonia

The points to note are that:

(a)   speech of reduced volume, with a cough of gradual onset (bovine cough), occurs with vocal cord paralysis (note that a normal cough has an explosive onset); and

(b)   reduced volume with a normal cough suggests a local laryngeal problem or functional (hysterical) dysphonia.

Dysarthria

The features of any dysarthria depend on the location of the lesion.

• Upper motor neurone lesions result in pseudobulbar palsy

The patient's speech is slow, slurred, monotonous and high-pitched and is often described as 'Donald Duck' dysarthria. The tongue has limited protrusion, is small and contracted and lies on the floor of the mouth. Palatal movements may be absent. The jaw jerk is exaggerated and there may be emotional lability.

• Lower motor neurone lesions result in bulbar palsy

The patient's speech is usually indistinct and

Table 2.6
Types of dysphasia.

Type of dysphasia	Comprehension	Fluency	Repetition	Naming
Wernicke's (receptive or sensory)	Abnormal	Fluent	Abnormal	Abnormal
Broca's (expressive or motor)	Good	Non-fluent	Abnormal	Abnormal
Global	Abnormal	Non-fluent	Abnormal	Abnormal
Transcortical sensory	Abnormal	Fluent	Good	Abnormal
Transcortical motor	Good	Non-fluent	Good	Abnormal
Conduction	Good	Fluent	Abnormal	Abnormal
Nominal (anomic)	Good	Fluent	Good	Abnormal

slurred and, in cases of bilateral paralysis of the palate, it has a nasal twang. The tongue develops wasting and fasciculation, and there may be accompanying weakness of the facial muscles.

• Extrapyramidal lesions
In Parkinson's disease, the patient's speech is often described as monotonous because it is slow, low-pitched and without inflection. The words are slurred and often trailed at the end of sentences.

• Cerebellar lesions (ataxic dysarthria)
In ataxic dysarthria, the patient's speech is slow, slurred and scanning. (Individual words are broken down into syllables and spoken with varying force).

• Myopathies and neuromuscular junction disorders

Speech in these disorders is similar to that in bulbar palsy. In myasthenia gravis, a well known neuromuscular junction disorder, there is evidence of fatigability since the dysarthria worsens during the course of the day.

Dysphasia

Dysphasias can be classified in a variety of ways (e.g. expressive (motor) and receptive (sensory), or fluent and non-fluent). Clinically, the latter way of classifying dysphasias is more useful because it is based on the patient's speech. The distinctive features of the different types of dysphasia are summarized in *Table 2.6*, and an overview of the causes is provided in diagrammatic form using a simplified model of speech in *Fig. 2.3*.

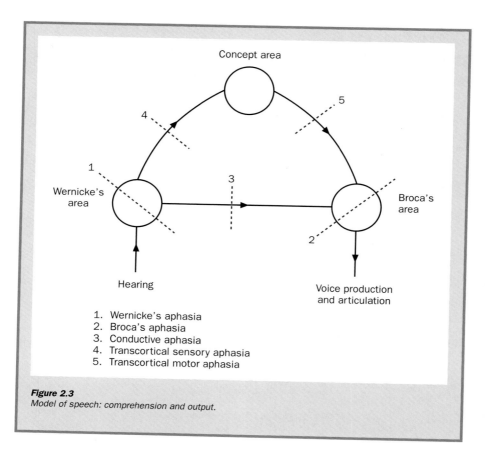

Concept area

Wernicke's area

Broca's area

Hearing

Voice production and articulation

1. Wernicke's aphasia
2. Broca's aphasia
3. Conductive aphasia
4. Transcortical sensory aphasia
5. Transcortical motor aphasia

Figure 2.3
Model of speech: comprehension and output.

Cranial nerves

Cranial nerve I (olfactory nerve)

Functional anatomy

Olfactory receptors in the nasal mucosa transmit signals along primary neurones, which pass via the ethmoidal cribriform plate to form synapses with olfactory bulb secondary neurones. The axons of these olfactory bulb secondary neurones pass along the olfactory tract and lateral olfactory striae to reach the primary olfactory area. This is then connected to the olfactory association area via tertiary neurones.

Examination

Most neurologists rarely test the olfactory nerve. It is only tested if the patient complains of a change in smell or taste. If an examination is indicated, each nostril should be tested separately using readily identifiable odiferous substances.

Interpretation of examination

Anosmia is the complete loss of the sense of smell whereas hyposmia, the more usual situation, is a diminished sense of smell. These conditions occur either because the odour is unable to reach the olfactory receptors or because olfactory nerve neurotransmission is interrupted. However, occasionally anosmia is 'psychogenic'. In such cases, patients fail to respond even to irritative substances such as ammonia, which normally stimulates trigeminal nerve receptors and should therefore still be sensed. It is also of interest to note that partial complex seizures originating from the uncus of the temporal lobe (uncinate fits) can generate olfactory hallucinations, which usually manifest themselves as transient sweet smells.

Cranial nerve II (optic nerve)

Functional anatomy

The visual pathways are summarized in *Fig. 2.4*, which also shows the sites of potential lesions.

Examination

Testing of the optic nerve is conveniently divided into several smaller examinations. A comprehensive examination is rarely necessary, but, at the very least, the basic components of each test should be performed.

Complete clinical assessment involves:

(a) assessing the visual acuity of both eyes;
(b) mapping their visual fields;
(c) testing them for colour vision;
(d) performing fundoscopy on each eye; and
(e) eliciting their pupillary responses.

- **Visual acuity**

Visual acuity is examined using specialized charts:

(a) the Snellen chart; and
(b) near-vision charts.

The patient is asked to read lines of letters on a Snellen chart from a distance of 6 m. Refractive errors are corrected with lenses or by looking through a pinhole before testing. Each eye is tested individually and the visual acuity is expressed as a fraction (e.g. $\frac{6}{6}$ or $\frac{6}{18}$). The numerator denotes the distance between the patient and the chart, and the denominator denotes the smallest size of letters that the patient can accurately read. Therefore a visual acuity of $\frac{6}{18}$ indicates that at 6 m, the patient can only read letters that a

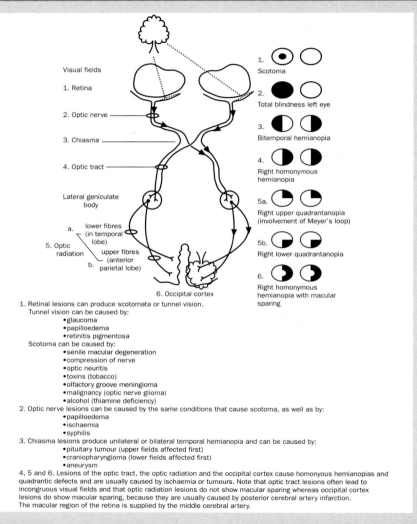

Visual fields

1. Retina

2. Optic nerve

3. Chiasma

4. Optic tract

Lateral geniculate body

5. Optic radiation
  a. lower fibres (in temporal lobe)
  b. upper fibres (anterior parietal lobe)

6. Occipital cortex

1. Scotoma

2. Total blindness left eye

3. Bitemporal hemianopia

4. Right homonymous hemianopia

5a. Right upper quadrantanopia (involvement of Meyer's loop)

5b. Right lower quadrantanopia

6. Right homonymous hemianopia with macular sparing

1. Retinal lesions can produce scotomata or tunnel vision.
   Tunnel vision can be caused by:
   - glaucoma
   - papilloedema
   - retinitis pigmentosa
   Scotoma can be caused by:
   - senile macular degeneration
   - compression of nerve
   - optic neuritis
   - toxins (tobacco)
   - olfactory groove meningioma
   - malignancy (optic nerve glioma)
   - alcohol (thiamine deficiency)
2. Optic nerve lesions can be caused by the same conditions that cause scotoma, as well as by:
   - papilloedema
   - ischaemia
   - syphilis
3. Chiasma lesions produce unilateral or bilateral temporal hemianopia and can be caused by:
   - pituitary tumour (upper fields affected first)
   - craniopharyngioma (lower fields affected first)
   - aneurysm
4, 5 and 6. Lesions of the optic tract, the optic radiation and the occipital cortex cause homonyous hemianopias and quadrantic defects and are usually caused by ischaemia or tumours. Note that optic tract lesions often lead to incongruous visual fields and that optic radiation lesions do not show macular sparing whereas occipital cortex lesions do show macular sparing, because they are usually caused by posterior cerebral artery infarction. The macular region of the retina is supplied by the middle cerebral artery.

Figure 2.4
Visual pathways showing sites of lesions and resulting visual field defects.

person with normal vision would be able to read at 18 m. If none of the letters on a Snellen chart can be read, then it should be brought closer. If, however, the letters still cannot be perceived, then the ability of the patient to count fingers, detect hand movement or perceive light should be recorded.

On a near-vision chart, the patient is asked to read sections of print from a distance of 30 cm. The smallest print size that can be read is recorded (e.g. N6).

Interpretation of examination

Visual acuity can be diminished because of lesions anywhere along the visual pathway between the cornea and the visual cortex.

- **Visual fields**

Visual field testing can be performed to varying degrees of thoroughness, depending on the extent to which a defect is suspected.

If a simple assessment is sought, when there is a low index of suspicion, the following abbreviated technique will suffice. Sitting opposite the patient, approximately 1 m away (confrontation technique), ask him or her to focus the gaze on the bridge of your nose. Extend both your arms above the visual horizontal axis in order to test the upper half of the visual fields, and quickly move the index fingers of each hand once, having asked the patient to report any movement that he or she may perceive. This is then repeated below the visual horizontal axis to test the lower half of the visual fields.

Detailed visual field testing is necessary if the patient complains of visual symptoms or if a specific defect is suspected. Each eye is tested individually using the confrontation technique. A white pinhead is used for screening peripheral visual field defects, and a red pinhead is used to assess central vision. This is because white objects are more easily seen than red objects and because central vision, which uses cones, is in colour whereas peripheral vision, which uses rods, is monochrome. The patient is asked to shut the right eye and to look with the left eye straight into the examiner's right eye (for comparison, the examiner's left eye is also shut). A pinhead is then introduced into the field of vision at a point mid-way between the patient and the examiner from several different directions, and each time the patient should report its appearance as soon as it is detected. In this manner the visual fields for both eyes are mapped and, if a field defect is found, the edges are carefully defined. Note that when a red pinhead is used the patient is asked to report not when the pin is first seen but when it is first perceived as red. By using a small red pinhead and moving it laterally along the horizontal meridian, the blind spot can also be mapped by asking the patient to identify when the pinhead disappears and then reappears.

Interpretation of examination

A monocular visual field defect is indicative of ocular, retinal or optic nerve damage. A visual defect affecting both eyes is suggestive of an optic chiasm lesion or a more proximal prechiasmal lesion. *Figure 2.4* summarizes the visual field defects and their usual causes.

- **Colour vision**

Testing for colour vision involves reading Ishihara plates, which have coloured dots arranged in such a way that a number is hidden within the pattern. Defects of colour vision can occur because of acquired disease of the visual pathways, or because of an inherited condition, such as X-linked colour blindness.

- **Fundoscopy**

Fundoscopy, the examination of the retina, is best performed in a dark room so that the pupils are enabled to dilate.

The patient is asked to stare at a fixed point in the distance. Then, with the right hand holding the ophthalmoscope, the examiner approaches the patient's right eye from the patient's right side at an angle of about 15° and a distance of 30 cm. This procedure is then repeated in reverse for the left eye.

During fundoscopy, the eye is also tested for the red reflex, and the optic disc and retinal blood vessels are examined for abnormalities.

Interpretation of examination

Fundoscopy is used to detect the effects on the retina of a wide range of general medical conditions, such as diabetes mellitus and hypertension. It is an important examination that requires skill, and it provides a considerable amount of useful information. The main objective of fundoscopy is to inspect the optic disc, abnormalities of which fall into two perceivable patterns:

(a) optic atrophy; and
(b) optic disc swelling.

Optic atrophy

In optic atrophy there is pallor of the optic disc because of atrophy of the nerve fibres. It occurs most commonly because of acquired disorders such as glaucoma, ischaemia, demyelination and trauma, but it can also be observed in rare hereditary diseases such as Friedreich's ataxia. Chronic papilloedema and metabolic disturbances such as vitamin B_{12} deficiency also produce optic atrophy, as does toxic alcohol consumption.

Optic disc swelling

Optic disc swelling can occur because of papilloedema or papillitis. As the optic disc swells, its margins become blurred and it is sometimes surrounded by haemorrhages. Papilloedema is the result of raised intracranial pressure that is transmitted to the optic nerve sheath, whereas papillitis is the result of inflammatory processes that involve the optic nerve near the retina. The two can normally be distinguished by assessing visual acuity and central vision, because in papillitis visual acuity is affected relatively early in the course of the disease and is associated with a central scotoma, whereas in papilloedema visual acuity is affected much later. Furthermore, papillitis usually involves only one eye whereas papilloedema usually affects both eyes (see *Table 2.7*).

- **Pupillary responses**

Anatomy

- The light reflex

When light shines into the eye, an afferent impulse passes from the retina to the optic nerve and the optic tract. Fibres concerned with the light reflex project to the pretectal nucleus of the mid-brain. From the pretectal region, fibres pass to the ipsilateral and contralateral Edinger–Westphal nuclei. The Edinger–Westphal nuclei give rise to preganglionic fibres, which pass via the oculomotor nerve to the ciliary ganglion. From the ciliary ganglion, postganglionic parasympathetic fibres innervate the iris sphincter pupillae (which constrict the pupil) and the ciliary body on each side (*Fig. 2.5*). Therefore, shining a light into either eye results in equal constriction of both pupils. These are termed the direct (same eye) and consensual (other eye) responses.

Table 2.7
Causes of papilloedema.

---

1) *Raised intracranial pressure:*
   Space occupying lesions e.g. tumours, haematomas
   Cerebral oedema e.g. due to infarction.
   Obstructive hydrocephalus.
   Infections e.g. meningitis, encephalitis.
   Venous sinus thrombosis.
   Idiopathic intracranial hypertension.
2) *Medical disorders:*
   Severe anaemia.
   Polycythaemia rubra vera.
   Accelerated hypertension.
   Toxins e.g. lead poisoning.
   Metabolic causes e.g. carbon dioxide retention.
   Drugs e.g. tetracycline, excess vitamin A intake.

Causes of Papillitis:
   Multiple sclerosis.
   Infections e.g. tuberculosis, bacterial meningitis.
   Inflammation of the orbit.

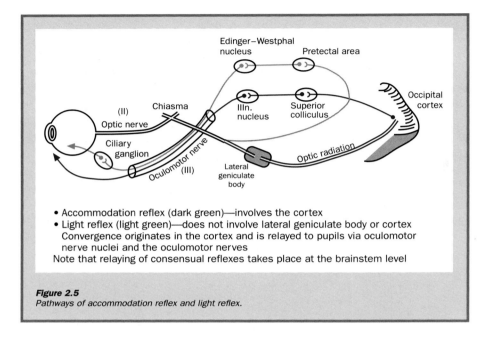

- Accommodation reflex (dark green)—involves the cortex
- Light reflex (light green)—does not involve lateral geniculate body or cortex
  Convergence originates in the cortex and is relayed to pupils via oculomotor
  nerve nuclei and the oculomotor nerves
Note that relaying of consensual reflexes takes place at the brainstem level

Figure 2.5
Pathways of accommodation reflex and light reflex.

- The accommodation reflex
When looking at nearby objects, the eyes accommodate. This involves convergence and constriction of the pupils and an increase in the refractive power by virtue of the lenses becoming thicker as the ciliary bodies contract. This reflex—the accommodation reflex—is thought to involve the parieto-occipital cortex, from where projections to the Edinger–Westphal nuclei mediate pupillary constriction, and projections to the mid-brain oculomotor nuclei, which mediate convergence (see *Fig. 2.5*).

Examination
The first step is to inspect the pupils, noting their shape and size. The light and accommodation reflexes of each eye are then tested using a pen-torch.

To test the pupillary light response, a bright light is shone into one eye and the reaction of both pupils (direct and consensual reflexes) is noted as being present, sluggish or absent.

In the swinging light test, a bright light is shone repeatedly into one eye and then the other, alternating between the two every

Table 2.8
The small, constricted (miotic) pupil.

Cause	Light reflex	Accommodation reflex	Other features
Senile	Normal	Normal	Bilateral small pupils Elderly
Horner's syndrome	Normal	Normal	Ptosis Enophthalmos Anhydrosis
Argyll–Robertson pupils	Absent	Normal	Irregular pupils Usually bilateral
Pontine lesion	Absent	Absent	Bilateral pin-point pupils in a comatose patient suggests an intrapontine lesion
Miotic drugs	Absent	Absent	Differential diagnosis for pontine lesion

1–2 seconds. During this time the pupillary responses are noted. Failure of the afferent visual pathway (retinal, optic nerve, optic chiasma or optic tract lesion) will result in the pupil of the affected eye repeatedly dilating and constricting. This is because the pupil constricts in response to an intact consensual input from the unaffected eye but dilates when light is shone into it, since the afferent component of the direct reflex is absent. The pupil of a normal eye remains constricted throughout the test, since this is achieved alternately via the direct and consensual pupillary light reflexes.

To test the accommodation reflex, the patient is asked to look into the distance and then at a finger positioned 10 cm directly in front of his or her nose. The pupils are examined as the patient attempts to focus on the finger and reaction of the pupils to accommodation is noted.

Interpretation of examination
The interpretation of the pupillary responses is presented in *Tables 2.8* and *2.9*. Anisocoria describes unequal sized pupils that are found as a normal variant in 20% of the population. The pupillary responses are unaltered.

Table 2.9
The large, dilated (mydriatic) pupil.

Cause	Light reflex	Accommodation reflex	Other features
Afferent light reflex pathway	Slow and incomplete or totally absent in affected eye; normal in unaffected eye	Normal	Swinging light test abnormal
Oculomotor nerve lesion	Absent	Absent	Ptosis 'Down and out' eye
Mid-brain lesion	Absent	Absent	Bilateral semidilated pupils Impaired vertical gaze
Holmes–Adie pupil	Responds very slowly	Responds slowly	Absent ankle jerks Impaired sweating Young females
Mydriatic drugs (e.g. atropine, adrenaline)	Absent	Absent	

Cranial nerves III (oculomotor nerve), IV (trochlear nerve) and VI (abducens nerve)

Conjugate eye movements

Conjugate gaze is the synchronous movement of both eyes. There are three types of eye movements involved in conjugate gaze (*Fig. 2.6*).

(a) saccadic eye movements, which are the rapid simultaneous movements that enable the fixation of new images on to the macula. They are under voluntary control and are initiated in the frontal lobes;

(b) pursuit eye movements, which are slow and smooth and are used to maintain fixation of a moving image on the

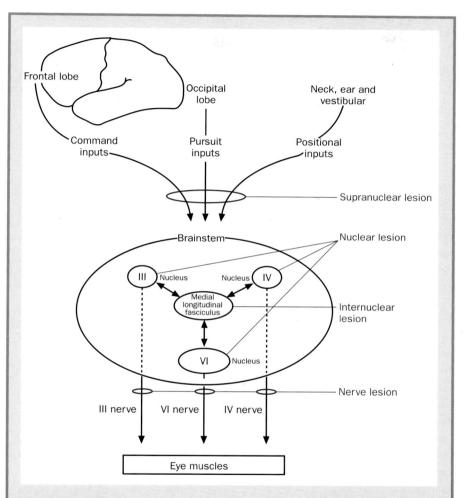

Figure 2.6
The control of eye movements. Adapted from Fuller G. Neurological examination made easy.
(Edinburgh: Churchill Livingstone, 1996)

macula. They are controlled by the parieto-occipital lobe in close liaison with the visual cortex; and

(c) positional eye movements, which are those that adjust and compensate for positional changes of the head in space. They are controlled by vestibular and cerebellar nuclei.

The inputs from these pathways are integrated in the brainstem and involve the paramedian pontine reticular formation and the medial longitudinal fasciculus (see *Fig. 2.6*). The paramedian pontine reticular formation is a structure in the pons that is the centre for horizontal gaze. Projections to the abducens nucleus mediate abduction via the lateral rectus muscle. Projections via the medial longitudinal fasciculus to the contralateral oculomotor nucleus mediate adduction of the contralateral eye via the medial rectus muscle. The medial longitudinal fasciculus runs between the mid-brain oculomotor and trochlear nerve nuclei and the pontine nucleus of the abducens nerve. These structures have inputs to the oculomotor, trochlear and abducens cranial nerve nuclei, which in turn innervate the eye muscles as follows (*Fig. 2.7*):

(a) the trochlear nerve supplies the superior oblique muscle;

(b) the abducens nerve supplies the lateral rectus muscle; and

(c) the oculomotor nerve innervates all the remaining extraocular muscles, and it also carries the parasympathetic fibres to the sphincter pupillae and the nerve supply to the levator palpebrae superioris, which elevates the eyelids.

Convergence

Convergence is the co-ordinated movement of both eyes towards fixation on the same near point.

Examination

Note the primary position of the head and then examine the eyelids for ptosis and the eyes for any squints (note the primary position of the eyes).

• Pursuit eye movements

Test pursuit eye movements by holding a finger about an arm's length from the patient (to avoid strain on convergence) and asking for it to be followed solely with the eyes (i.e. without any head movement). Slowly move the finger horizontally and vertically in the centre of the visual field and at the extremes of lateral gaze while keenly observing the patient's eye movements. Inform the patient to report the occurrence of double vision (diplopia).

• Saccadic eye movements

Test saccadic eye movements by asking the

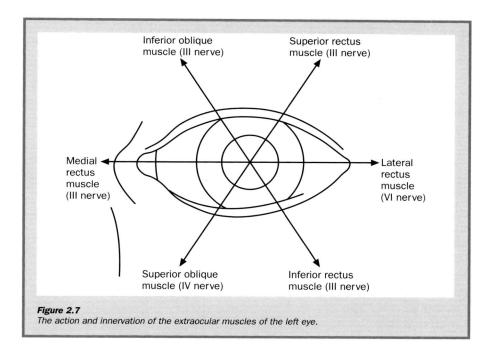

Figure 2.7
The action and innervation of the extraocular muscles of the left eye.

patient to swiftly look to the right, left, up and down while observing the eyes.

• Convergence

Test convergence by asking the patient to look into the distance and then to fixate on a target as it is gradually brought closer from a distance of 50 cm to the limit of convergence.

There are several special tests that can be used.

• Cover test

The patient is asked to fixate on a distant target with both eyes, and while the patient does this the left eye is covered with a piece of card. While continuing to maintain fixation, the left eye is quickly uncovered to cover the right eye instead. During this switch, the left eye is closely observed to determine whether its position is corrected so as to maintain fixation. The test is then repeated on the right eye. Normally, eye positions do not change

Table 2.10
Causes of ptosis.

Unilateral ptosis	Third nerve palsy
	Horner's syndrome
	Myasthenia gravis
	Congenital or idiopathic ptosis
Bilateral ptosis	Myasthenia gravis
	Muscular dystrophy (e.g. myotonic dystrophy, oculopharyngeal dystrophy)
	Ocular myopathy
	Neurosyphilis (tabes dorsalis)
	Bilateral Horner's syndrome
	Mitochondrial disorders
	Congenital ptosis

when the eye is covered and uncovered. This test is used to detect a non-paralytic squint (see page 31) in which one eye has to correct as it is uncovered.

• Vestibulo-ocular reflex
Naturally, the above method cannot be used in an unconscious patient. In such instances, brainstem pathways, particularly those involving the vestibular nuclei, can be assessed using the doll's eye manoeuvre or the caloric test.

The doll's eye manoeuvre involves turning the patient's head from side to side, followed by flexing and then extending the neck. Normally the eyes should move within the orbits so as to maintain forward gaze.

The caloric test is described under the vestibulocochlear nerve (see page 43).

• Optokinetic nystagmus
See nystagmus under vestibulocochlear nerve (page 40).

Interpretation of the tests
• Head tilt
Usually the head is tilted away from the side of a trochlear nerve lesion.

• Ptosis
Ptosis denotes drooping of the upper eyelids. It can be unilateral or bilateral and has many causes, some of which are given in *Table 2.10*.

• Strabismus
Strabismus, or squint, is the misalignment of the visual axes. Binocular vision requires light from an image to fall on corresponding parts

of the two retinae. This is then fused into a single image by the brain. If the visual axes of the eyes become misaligned, then the patient develops a squint. The main types of squint are described below.

A comitant (non-paralytic) squint occurs as a result of increased tone in one ocular muscle compared with its synergist. It is usually congenital, and the patient learns to ignore or suppress one image before the central connections of the visual system are fully developed, and therefore there is no diplopia. The squint remains constant in all directions of gaze, although both eyes have full movement if tested separately. The cover test is abnormal and visual acuity is reduced in the affected eye.

A non-comitant (paralytic) squint is usually an acquired squint in which the degree of misalignment varies with the direction of gaze and the patient experiences diplopia.

• Diplopia ('double vision')

In diplopia, the patient perceives two images, of which the false image is always peripheral and seen by the affected eye. Separation of the two images is maximal in the direction of action of the affected muscle.

The causes of diplopia include:

(a) oculomotor, trochlear and abducens nuclei or nerve lesions;

(b) neuromuscular junction disorders (e.g. myasthenia gravis);

(c) muscle disorders (e.g. ocular myopathy, thyroid disorders); and

(d) orbital lesions (e.g. retro-orbital arteriovenous malformation or tumour).

Supranuclear and internuclear lesions generally do not result in diplopia.

IIIrd (oculomotor) nerve palsy

In an oculomotor nerve palsy, there is usually ptosis. The pupil may be dilated and completely non-reactive. The eye is abducted (by the lateral rectus muscle) and depressed (by the superior oblique muscle) (i.e. the eye is 'down and out'). (See *Table 2.11*).

IVth (trochlear) nerve palsy

In a trochlear nerve palsy, there is failure of downward movement and gaze when the eye is adducted (which the patient notes when walking down steps). Diplopia occurs on looking downwards and medially, and, since the two images are at an angle, the patient tilts the head to compensate for this. (See *Table 2.11*).

VIth (abducens) nerve palsy

An abducens nerve palsy causes failure of eye abduction, which leads to diplopia

Table 2.11
Causes of IIIrd, IVth and VIth nerve palsies.

Mononeuritis multiplex (e.g. diabetes
  mellitus, vasculitis)
Hypertension or raised intracranial
  pressure
Brainstem infarction
Tumours
Multiple sclerosis with a brainstem
  demyelinating lesion
Trauma

with parallel real and false images on lateral
gaze. (See *Table 2.11*).

Horizontal gaze palsies

Horizontal gaze palsies can occur because of:

(a) destructive frontal lobe lesions, which
     cause deviation of the eyes to the
     ipsilateral side and hemiparesis on the
     contralateral side;

(b) pontine lesions, which lead to ipsilateral
     deviation of the eyes and hemiparesis;
     and

(c) medial longitudinal fasciculus lesions
     (internuclear ophthalmoplegia), in
     which the eye fails to adduct on
     attempting lateral gaze towards the side
     of the lesion. This is often accompanied

by a coarse (ataxic) nystagmus in the
abducting eye. A bilateral internuclear
ophthalmoplegia is almost pathognomic
of multiple sclerosis.

Vertical gaze palsies

Vertical gaze palsies are caused by upper
brainstem lesions and certain degenerative
disorders (e.g. progressive supranuclear palsy).

Abnormal saccadic eye movements

In normal saccadic eye movements, the
eyes move rapidly and smoothly to fixate on
a new target. Saccades that overshoot are
called hypermetric whereas those that
undershoot are called hypometric. Abnormal
saccadic eye movements indicate a cerebellar
lesion.

Nystagmus

See page 40.

Cranial nerve V (trigeminal nerve)

Anatomy

The anatomy of the trigeminal nerve is
presented in *Fig. 2.8*.

Examination

The trigeminal nerve is the largest cranial
nerve and has several components, each of
which needs to be tested separately.

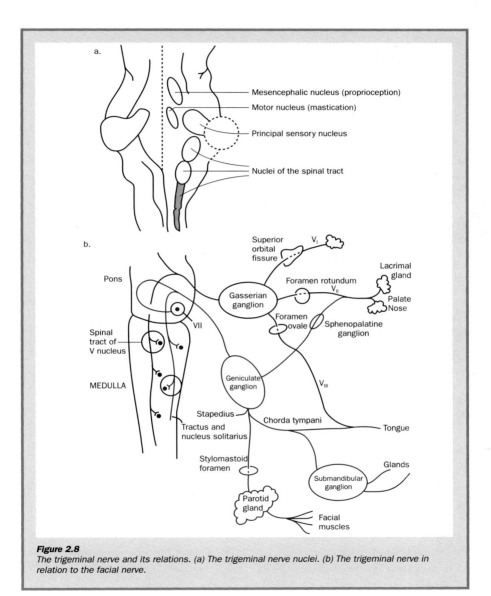

Figure 2.8
The trigeminal nerve and its relations. (a) The trigeminal nerve nuclei. (b) The trigeminal nerve in relation to the facial nerve.

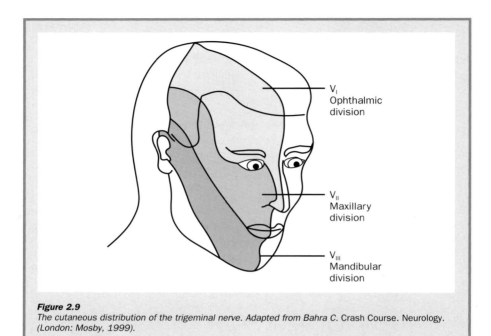

Figure 2.9
The cutaneous distribution of the trigeminal nerve. Adapted from Bahra C. Crash Course. Neurology.
(London: Mosby, 1999).

V₁ Ophthalmic division

V₁₁ Maxillary division

V₁₁₁ Mandibular division

Facial sensation

The cutaneous distribution of the trigeminal nerve and its three divisions is shown in *Fig. 2.9*. Test light touch and pinprick in each division of the nerve on both sides, comparing one side with the other. If any abnormality is found then also test temperature sensation. The findings should be interpreted as follows:

(a) loss of all modalities in one or two of the divisions indicates a possible lesion either of the Gasserian ganglion or of a division of the trigeminal nerve during its intracranial course;

(b) loss of sensation of all modalities in all divisions indicates a lesion of the Gasserian ganglion, sensory root or sensory nucleus;

(c) loss of light touch alone indicates a pontine sensory root lesion, and hemisensory loss of light touch further suggests a contralateral parietal lobe lesion;

(d) loss of pinprick and temperature sensation along with contralateral loss of these modalities on the body indicates an ipsilateral brainstem lesion; and

(e) sensory loss around the mouth suggests a lesion of the descending spinal sensory nucleus (e.g. due to syringomyelia).

Motor component

• The muscles of mastication

Inspect the temples for wasting of the temporalis muscles and then palpate these and the masseters when the teeth are clenched. The patient is then asked to open the mouth against resistance from the examiner's hand, which should be placed firmly under the patient's chin. Any deviation of the jaw is noted. The findings should be interpreted as follows:

(a) wasting of the temporalis and masseter muscles is found in myotonic dystrophy, motor neurone disease and facioscapulohumeral dystrophy; and

(b) jaw deviation is indicative of a unilateral lesion of the trigeminal nerve motor component that innervates the ipsilateral pterygoid muscle.

• The jaw jerk

With the patient's mouth slightly open, the relaxed chin is tapped, indirectly, using a percussion hammer. When the jaw jerk is normal there is usually minimal movement of the jaw. A brisk jaw jerk indicates an upper motor neurone lesion with localization of the lesion to above the foramen magnum.

• The corneal reflex

Cotton wool that has been twisted to form a point is used to touch the cornea (not the sclera) while the patient looks up and away from the examiner. Observe both eyes blink. A bilaterally absent blink response suggests a lesion of the ophthalmic division (V_1) of the trigeminal nerve. Unilateral absence suggests ipsilateral facial palsy. A subjective reduction in corneal sensation suggests a partial V_1 lesion. For the causes of trigeminal nerve palsy, please refer to *Table 2.12*.

Cranial nerve VII (facial nerve)

Anatomy

The facial nerve has sensory, parasympathetic and motor nuclei that:

(a) innervate the muscles of facial expression, the tensor tympani and the stapedius;

(b) carry taste sensation from the anterior two-thirds of the tongue (carried in the

Table 2.12
Causes of trigeminal nerve palsy according to the site of the lesion.

Site of lesion	Cause
Brainstem (nuclei and central connections)	Infarction Multiple sclerosis Syringobulbia Tumour (e.g. glioma, metastatic deposits)
Cerebellopontine angle	Acoustic neuroma Meningioma Metastatic deposits
Cavernous sinus	Cavernous sinus thrombosis Aneurysm of the internal carotid artery Tumour (e.g. extension of pituitary tumour, metastasis deposit)
Apex of petrous temporal bone	Gradenigo's syndrome (associated with abducens nerve palsy and results from chronic middle ear infection) Tumour of the petrous temporal bone
Trigeminal root, ganglion and peripheral branch	Herpes zoster infection Tumour Granulomatous disease (e.g. tuberculosis, sarcoidosis) Vasculitis (e.g. systemic lupus erythematosus) Trigeminal neuralgia

chorda tympani, a branch of the facial nerve); and

(c) are involved in salivation and lacrimation.

The sensory portion of the facial nerve also supplies the external auditory canal up to the tragus of the ear.

Examination

Motor component
Inspect the face carefully, looking for any asymmetry or abnormal movements, especially with changes of emotion. The facial muscles can be formally tested by asking the patient to raise the eyebrows, close the eyes

Table 2.13
Causes of facial nerve lesions.

	Lower motor neurone lesion	*Upper motor neurone lesion*

Unilateral lesion	Idiopathic Bell's palsy
	Pons (e.g. infarction, demyelination,
	    tumour deposits)
	Cerebellopontine angle
	Facial canal (e.g. middle ear infection,
	    tumour, fracture of skull base)
	Geniculate ganglions (e.g. herpes
	    zoster infection)
	Peripheral branches of the nerve
	    (e.g. parotid gland lesions such as
	    tumour, sarcoidosis, infection;
	    or trauma)
		Stroke
		Demyelination
		Tumours

Bilateral lesion	Sarcoidosis Guillain–Barré syndrome Bilateral Bell's palsy Myasthenia gravis Myopathies (e.g. myotonic dystrophy, fascioscapulohumeral dystrophy	Pseudobulbar palsy Motor neurone disease

tightly, blow out the cheeks, show the teeth and purse the lips tightly.

Taste

Taste is rarely tested in clinical practice. A cotton bud is dipped into a sweet, salty, bitter or sour solution and applied to the tongue. The patient is asked to identify each solution, and the mouth is rinsed with distilled water between tests. Each side of the anterior two-thirds and posterior one-third of the tongue is tested separately.

Cutaneous sensation

Although the facial nerve has a small cutaneous distribution around the ears, the overlap with adjacent nerves is such that testing this function is not useful.

Interpretation of examination

An expressionless face with normal muscle strength is seen in patients with Parkinsonism. It does not indicate bilateral facial palsy. Exclusive weakness of the lower face muscles suggests a contralateral upper motor neurone (supranuclear) lesion. This may be accompanied by ipsilateral hemiplegia. Weakness of both the upper and lower halves of the face is due to a lower motor neurone lesion (i.e. a disorder of the facial nucleus, the geniculate ganglion, the peripheral facial nerve, the neuromuscular junction or muscle).

Bell's phenomenon describes an automatic attempt to cover the cornea by rolling the eyeball outwards and upwards when attempting to keep the eyes shut. Please refer to *Table 2.13* for causes of facial nerve lesions.

Cranial nerve VIII (vestibulocochlear nerve)

The vestibulocochlear nerve has two functional divisions:

(a)   the cochlear nerve, which mediates hearing; and
(b)   the vestibular nerve, which maintains balance.

Hearing

To test hearing, each ear is tested individually by blocking the opposite ear. Initially, test hearing sensitivity to a whispered sound or a ticking wristwatch. If hearing is reduced in either ear, then perform Rinne's test and Weber's test.

Rinne's test

Rinne's test compares bone conduction with air conduction. Hold the stem of a vibrating 512 Hz tuning fork firmly over the patient's mastoid process until the patient reports that the buzzing sound has disappeared. Then immediately place the fork in front of the patient's ear. Ask the patient if the buzzing can still be heard. Normally, it is still possible at this time to detect the vibrations when the tuning fork is held in front of the ear (i.e. conduction through air is better than that through bone). This is referred to as a positive result.

Weber's test

Place the stem of a vibrating 512 Hz tuning fork over the vertex or on the forehead in the midline. Ask the patient in which ear the vibrating sound is louder. Normally, the sound is heard equally loudly in both ears. With conduction deafness the sound is louder in the affected ear, whereas with nerve deafness the sound is louder in the normal ear.

Interpretation of hearing tests

Rinne's and Weber's tests help to distinguish between conductive and sensorineural deafness (*Table 2.14*). Conductive deafness is caused by a lesion of the sound-conducting apparatus (i.e. external and middle ear disease) (*Table 2.15*). Sensorineural deafness is caused by a lesion of the sensory mechanism of the ear (the cochlea), the cochlear nerve or its central connection (*Table 2.16*).

Table 2.14
Hearing tests.

	Rinne's test	Weber's test
Conductive deafness	Negative (bone conduction better than air conduction)	Lateralizes to affected ear
Sensorineural deafness	Positive (air conduction better than bone conduction)	Lateralizes to unaffected or better ear

Table 2.15
Causes of conductive deafness.

Site of lesion	Cause
External auditory meatus (obstruction)	Wax Foreign body
Middle ear	Inflammation (e.g. otitis media) Trauma (e.g. rupture of the ear drum, dislocation of the ossicles) Otosclerosis Cholesteatoma

Table 2.16
Causes of sensorineural deafness.

Site of lesion	Cause
Cochlea	Ménière's disease Infection (e.g inner ear infection, meningitis) Drugs (e.g. aminoglycosides) Noise-induced damage Presbycusis
Cochlear nerve	Acoustic neuroma Basal meningitis Granulomatous disease Trauma
Cochlear nucleus	Brainstem infarction Multiple sclerosis Tumour

Balance

Gait

When walking, a patient veers towards the side of a vestibular lesion. (See Gait, page 66, for further details.)

Nystagmus

Nystagmus denotes the involuntary oscillatory movements of the eyes. Broadly speaking there are two types of nystagmus:

(a) jerk nystagmus, which is characterized by a slow movement in one direction followed by a fast corrective movement in the opposite direction (note that, by convention, the direction of nystagmus is that of the fast component); and

(b) pendular nystagmus, which is characterized by symmetrical movements in both directions.

The cause of nystagmus may be:

(a) physiological;
(b) retinal;
(c) peripheral (see *Table 2.17*);
(d) central (see *Table 2.17*).

• Physiological nystagmus
A fine nystagmus can occur at the extreme of lateral gaze or if eye movements are tested too fast (nystagmoid jerks). This is normal.

Optokinetic (jerk) nystagmus occurs when a cylinder with alternating black and white strips is rotated in front of a subject's eyes. The slow tracking eye movements, which represent normal pursuit movements to the limits of lateral conjugate gaze, are followed by fast corrective saccades with subsequent fixation on a new object in the visual field. Such movements are lost in unconscious patients and blind subjects, and therefore this is a useful test for detecting simulated disturbances of consciousness and non-organic blindness.

• Retinal causes of nystagmus
Pendular nystagmus occurs in cases of marked visual impairment or visual loss in early life (e.g. in albinism or with congenital cataracts) because of an inability to fixate.

• Peripheral causes of nystagmus
When nystagmus is due to a peripheral lesion, there is horizontal or rotary nystagmus, or both. The fast phase is in the opposite direction to the side of the lesion. Causes include:

(a) labyrinthine disease (e.g. benign positional vertigo, Meniere's disease, infection or trauma); and

(b) vestibular nerve lesion (e.g. trauma, an acoustic neuroma, infection with herpes zoster or vestibular neuronitis, which is thought to be postviral).

Table 2.17
Summary of peripheral and central nystagmus.

	Site of lesion	Nystagmus	Gait	Causes
Peripheral	Labyrinth	Horizontal and/or rotatory Fast phase opposite to lesion	Veers towards lesion	Benign positional vertigo Meniere's disease Infection Trauma
	Vestibular nerve	Horizontal and/or rotatory Fast phase opposite to lesion	Veers towards lesion	Vestibular neuronitis (thought to be postviral) Infection (herpes zoster) Acoustic neuroma Trauma
Central	Lesions of the vestibular nuclei and its connections	Horizontal, vertical and/ or rotatory	Veers towards lesion	Brainstem infarction Multiple sclerosis Tumour
	Cerebellar lesions	Horizontal Fast phase towards lesion	Ataxic gait towards lesion	See 'Co-ordination and cerebellar function' (page 55)

Table 2.18
Jerk nystagmus.

First-degree nystagmus	Present on lateral gaze with fast phase towards direction of gaze
Second-degree nystagmus	Present on forward gaze
Third-degree nystagmus	Present on lateral gaze with fast phase opposite to direction of gaze

- Central causes of nystagmus

Nystagmus caused by a central lesion may have a horizontal, vertical or rotatory component, or more than one of these. Causes include:

(a) lesions of the vestibular nuclei and its connections (e.g. brainstem infarction, multiple sclerosis or tumour); and

(b) cerebellar lesions, in which case there is horizontal nystagmus with the fast phase towards the side of the lesion and the patient's gait is ataxic with unsteadiness towards the side of the lesion.

Examination

Nystagmus is most likely to be noted when examining the eye movements described above (see page 30). If nystagmus is present, it is important to note the type (pendular or jerk nystagmus) and to assess whether it persists or fatigues, is associated with vertigo or improves with visual fixation. With jerk nystagmus, note the direction of the fast phase (horizontal, vertical or rotatory) and the position of the eye when the nystagmus occurs. This determines the degree of jerk nystagmus (*Table 2.18*).

Interpretation of tests

In order to distinguish between central and peripheral nystagmus, the following should be borne in mind.

- Jerk nystagmus

(a) pure rotatory nystagmus is due to central pathology, but peripheral horizontal nystagmus usually has a rotatory component;

(b) vertical nystagmus is always central in origin and is due to brainstem disease; upbeat nystagmus indicates upper brainstem disease, whereas downbeat nystagmus is characteristic of lesions at the foramen magnum; and

Table 2.19
Features of central and peripheral horizontal unidirectional nystagmus.

	Central	Peripheral
Duration	Sustained	Fatigues
Associated with vertigo	No	Yes
Effect of visual fixation	No effect	Reduces nystagmus

(c)   horizontal, unidirectional, first-degree nystagmus can be central or peripheral, whereas second- and third-degree nystagmus are usually central in origin; if it is peripheral then it is most likely to be acute and associated with vertigo.

To determine whether the lesion is central or peripheral the features in *Table 2.19* need to be noted.

(d)   Multidirectional gaze-evoked nystagmus
This type of nystagmus occurs in the direction of gaze but in more than one direction. It is always central in origin.

(e)   Ataxic nystagmus
Ataxic nystagmus is a horizontal, jerking nystagmus that is more prominent in the abducting eye than in the adducting eye. It occurs in association with incomplete adduction on lateral gaze (internuclear ophthalmoplegia) and is caused by a lesion of the medial longitudinal bundle.

Special tests
•   Caloric test
The caloric test is a test of vestibular function. It is normally performed in a laboratory because the patient may develop severe dizziness or nausea. Initially, the patient is asked to lie down on a bench with the head on a pillow at 30° and to look straight ahead. About 250 ml of cool (30°C) and warm water (44°C) are instilled over 40 seconds into each ear in turn while the eyes are observed.

The normal response is the development of nystagmus directed away from the ear with cold water and towards the ear with warm water. With pathology, the following results may be obtained:

(a)   canal paresis—reduced nystagmus to cold and warm water in one ear—which occurs in peripheral lesions such as labyrinthine lesions and vestibular nerve lesions; or

(b)   directional preponderance—reduced nystagmus in one direction (after ipsilateral warm stimulus and contralateral cold stimulus) compared with the other side—which occurs in vestibular nucleus lesions.

- Hallpike's test

Hallpike's test is used to test benign positional vertigo (i.e. transient vertigo precipitated by head movements). The patient is asked to sit upright on a flat bed so that if he or she were to lie down both the head and the neck would protrude over the edge. The head is then rotated to one side and the patient is asked to look towards the same side. The patient is then asked to lie back straight and the neck is extended by the examiner while supporting the head. The eyes are observed for nystagmus in the direction of gaze and to ascertain whether any such nystagmus is associated with delay and fatigability.

This test does normally result in nystagmus. A fatigable rotatory nystagmus with delay is indicative of peripheral vestibular disease (usually benign positional vertigo), whereas non-fatigable nystagmus without delay is indicative of central vestibular disease.

- Unterberger's test (turning test)

The patient is asked to hold both arms straight in front and walk on the spot. When doing this, the patient is then asked to close the eyes. At this point the patient's position should be observed—the patient will gradually turn towards the side of a vestibular lesion.

Cranial nerves IX (glossopharyngeal nerve) and X (vagus nerve)

Both the glossopharyngeal and vagus nerves have sensory, motor and autonomic components. The glossopharyngeal nerve supplies sensation to the posterior one-third of the tongue, the pharynx and the middle ear. It provides motor innervation to the stylopharyngeus muscle and autonomic innervation to the parotid gland. The vagus nerve supplies sensation to the tympanic membrane, the external auditory canal and the external ear. It provides motor innervation to the muscles of the palate, the larynx and the pharynx and autonomic innervation both to and from the thoracic and abdominal viscera.

Examination

Swallowing

Ask the patient to drink a few sips of water and swallow them. Observe for smooth co-ordination of actions and note whether swallowing is followed by coughing and spluttering.

Nasal regurgitation occurs with palatal incompetence caused by a vagus nerve lesion. Swallowing followed by coughing indicates aspiration caused by poor airway protection, and this also suggests a vagus nerve lesion.

Cough

Ask the patient to cough and note its quality. A normal cough has an explosive onset, whereas a cough with gradual onset (also called a bovine cough) occurs with vocal cord paralysis caused by vagus nerve lesions.

Speech

Test the patient's speech for dysarthria and dysphonia (see page 14).

Palatal movements

Ask the patient to say 'aah' and observe the uvula. Note that the soft palate normally moves upwards and the uvula maintains a central position throughout.

Minor and inconsistent deviations of the palate and uvula should generally be ignored; however, if on phonation the palate droops on one side and the uvula deviates to the contralateral side this is a sign of a unilateral, lower motor neurone, vagus nerve lesion on the same side as the palatal droop (i.e. contralateral to the direction of uvular deviation). Note that upper motor neurone innervation of palatal and pharyngeal muscles is bilateral and therefore unilateral upper motor neurone lesions do not cause significant dysfunction.

If the palate cannot be voluntarily elevated, this suggests bilateral upper or lower motor neurone vagus nerve lesions. These can be distinguished by eliciting the gag reflex, which is intact in bilateral upper motor neurone lesions (pseudobulbar palsy), but impaired in bilateral lower motor neurone lesions (bulbar palsy).

Gag reflex

Gently stimulate each side of the posterior pharyngeal wall by touching and observe the movements of the pharynx, palate and tongue.

The afferent arm of this reflex is via the glossopharyngeal nerve and the efferent arm is via the vagus nerve. Therefore, an absent gag reflex can result from lesions of either or both these nerves and their pathways (see Palatal movements, above).

Cranial nerve XI (accessory nerve)

The accessory nerve arises from the medulla and receives contributions from the cervical spinal roots of C2–C4. It innervates the sternocleidomastoid and trapezius muscles, with each cerebral hemisphere supplying the contralateral trapezius muscle and the ipsilateral sternocleidomastoid muscle.

Examination

Inspect the patient's neck and shoulder for wasting and fasciculation. Muscle strength is then tested, noting any pattern of weakness.

Test the sternocleidomastoid muscle by asking the patient to resist flexion of the neck. Observe the neck and shoulder muscles on both sides while doing this. Then ask the patient to turn the head in both directions against resistance, noting that the left sternocleidomastoid turns the head to the right and vice versa.

The trapezius muscles are then tested by asking the patient to shrug the shoulders against resistance.

Weakness of the ipsilateral sternocleidomastoid and trapezius muscles suggests a peripheral accessory nerve lesion, whereas weakness of the ipsilateral sternocleidomastoid and contralateral trapezius muscles suggests an ipsilateral upper motor neurone accessory nerve lesion. Bilateral weakness and wasting of the sternocleidomastoid muscles can be due to myopathy, such as occurs in myotonic muscular dystrophy or motor neurone disease. However, unilateral sternocleidomastoid muscle weakness is rare and usually post-traumatic.

Cranial nerve XII (hypoglossal nerve)

The hypoglossal nerve provides the motor supply to the muscles of the tongue

Examination

Initially the tongue is inspected as it lies on the floor of the mouth, noting any wasting, fasciculation and involuntary movement. The patient is then asked to stick out the tongue

and move it from side to side. Observations and their interpretations are summarized in *Table 2.20*.

Palsies of the lower four cranial nerves

Isolated palsies of the lower four cranial nerves (IX, X, XI and XII) are rare. Combined palsies are more common and the causes include:

(a) motor neurone disease;
(b) brainstem vascular disease;
(c) tumours of the brainstem, nasopharynx, skull base or glomus;
(d) polyneuropathy (e.g. Guillain–Barré syndrome);
(e) syringobulbia; and
(f) trauma.

Motor system

Anatomy

The normal motor function of muscles depends on the integrity of the higher motor centres, the upper and lower motor neurone pathways and the neuromuscular junction. The main motor pathway is the pyramidal tract, which has fibres descending from the motor complex to the cranial nerve nuclei in the brainstem and the anterior horn cells in the spinal cord (*Fig. 2.10*). From these, lower motor neurones innervate the muscles. Motor

Table 2.20
Examination of the hypoglossal nerve.

Inspection	Tongue protrusion	Interpretation
Unilateral wasting and fasciculations	Deviates to the side of wasting	Unilateral lower motor neurone lesion ipsilateral to the side to which the tongue deviates
Bilateral wasting and fasciculations	No deviation	Bilateral lower motor neurone lesion
Normal bulk, no fasciculations	Slight deviation of the tongue	Unilateral upper motor neurone contralateral to the side to which the tongue deviates
Appears contracted	Limited protrusion	Bilateral upper motor neurone lesion

function is modulated by inputs from the cerebellum and the extrapyramidal system and by sensory proprioceptive information.

Examination

To examine the motor function of the limbs it is necessary to:

(a)   inspect;
(b)   examine tone;
(c)   assess power;
(d)   test reflexes; and
(e)   evaluate co-ordination and gait.

Inspection

The following should be noted:

(a)   posture;
(b)   muscle wasting and fasciculations; and
(c)   involuntary movements.

Posture

Look for a hemiplegic posture, in which there is flexion of the elbow and wrist and extension of the knee and ankle. This characteristically occurs in upper motor neurone lesions. Ask the patient to hold both arms outstretched in front with the eyes closed, and observe for any drifting of the arms. Push each arm sharply up or down and observe the response. An outstretched arm drifting with pronation of the hand is called 'pronator drift', and this is a

feature of upper motor neurone lesions. Oscillation of an outstretched arm when the arm is suddenly displaced occurs with cerebellar disease.

Muscle wasting and fasciculations

Muscle wasting and fasciculations (brief, irregular twitching movements within the muscle belly that are often visible through the skin) are typically features of lower motor neurone lesions. Muscle wasting without fasciculations occurs in muscle disorders.

Involuntary movements

Involuntary movements are discussed in the chapter on Movement disorders (see page 109).

Tone

Tone is the resistance that occurs when a muscle is passively stretched. It is maintained by the activity of the stretch reflex (see *Fig. 2.11*). It is assessed in all four limbs with the patient's muscles relaxed.

To assess tone in the arm, hold the patient's arm and slowly flex and extend the elbow. Then, while holding the patient's hand and also supporting the elbow, pronate and supinate the patient's forearm. Finally, gently rotate the hand at the wrist.

To assess tone in the leg, rock the leg by the knees from side to side. Normally, the legs roll easily and the feet lag behind. Now, with

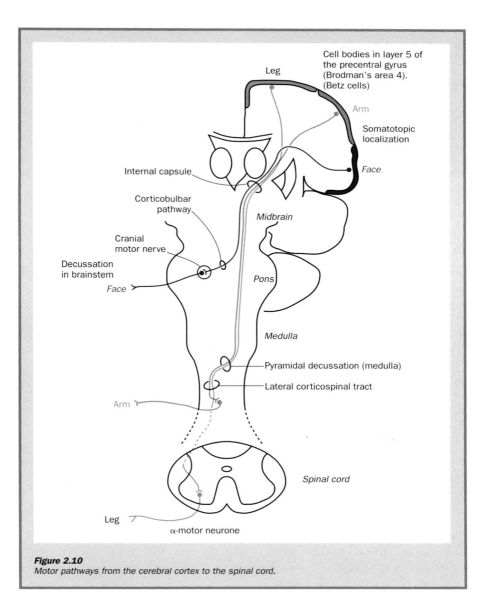

Figure 2.10
Motor pathways from the cerebral cortex to the spinal cord.

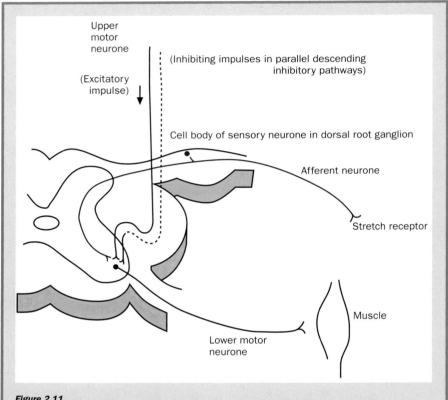

Figure 2.11
The stretch reflex. Note that the inhibitory descending pathways are involved in modulating the sensitivity of the stretch receptor.

the patient's legs extended, place your hand under the knee and rapidly lift it about 15 cm while observing the foot. Normally, the foot lifts only minimally off the bed. Then, holding the knee and ankle, extend and flex

the knee. Finally, holding the ankle and foot, plantarflex and dorsiflex the foot.

Clonus describes the rhythmic, unidirectional contractions evoked by a sudden passive stretch of a muscle. It is elicited most easily at the ankle or knee, and a few contractions are normal.

To examine for clonus at the ankle, with the knee slightly flexed, rapidly evert and dorsiflex the foot. To examine for clonus at the knee, place a hand just above the patient's knee cap such that the thumb lies on one side of it and the index finger on the other, then quickly push the knee cap downwards.

Interpretation of findings

Diminished muscle tone (hypotonia) describes a loss of resistance through movement, and so, for example, when examining leg tone, the heel is not lifted off the bed when the knee is lifted. This occurs with muscle disorders and in lower motor neurone and cerebellar lesions.

Increased tone leads to rigidity and spasticity. With lead-pipe rigidity, there is increased resistance throughout the range of movement, whereas with cogwheel rigidity, the increased tone is intermittent and ratchet-like and is essentially a combination of lead-pipe rigidity with superimposed tremor.

In spasticity there is also an increase in resistance throughout the range of movement, but this follows a sudden release—a 'catch'— and so, during an examination of leg tone, the heel lifts off the bed when the knee is lifted. This occurs in upper motor neurone lesions.

Rigidity is a feature of extrapyramidal disorders.

Related terms that deserve a mention include:

(a) gegenhalten, or paratonia, which is a sign of bilateral frontal lobe lesions and describes the patient's opposition to any attempted limb movements;

(b) myotonia, which is the delay in relaxation of muscle after contraction; it is usually seen in myotonic dystrophy; and

(c) dystonia, which is the contraction of both agonist and antagonist muscles, producing sustained abnormal limb postures; it is usually a feature of extrapyramidal disorders.

Power

Power is assessed by testing the patient's ability to contract the main muscle groups against gravity and then against resistance provided by the examiner. The power in each muscle group is graded using the Medical Research Council (MRC) scale (*Table 2.21*).

The schemes shown in *Fig. 2.12* allow testing of the major muscle groups. The tests are performed alternating from one side to the other so that the two sides can be compared.

Assessing muscle power in the upper limbs involves testing shoulder abduction, elbow extension and flexion, wrist extension and flexion, finger extension, flexion and abduction, and thumb abduction.

Assessing muscle power in the lower limbs involves testing hip flexion and extension,

Table 2.21
The MRC scale.

Grade	Response
0	No contraction
1	Flicker or trace of contraction
2	Active movement with gravity and resistance eliminated
3	Active movement against gravity but not against resistance
4	Active movement against both gravity and resistance but not full strength
5	Full strength

MRC, Medical Research Council.

knee flexion and extension, ankle dorsiflexion and plantar flexion.

Interpretation of findings

The patterns of weakness depend on the site of the pathology (see *Table 2.22*):

(a) upper motor neurone lesions;
(b) lower motor neurone lesions;
(c) neuromuscular junction disease; or
(d) myopathy.

Upper motor neurone lesions lead to weakness of muscle groups rather than of individual muscles. Weakness is most evident in the extensor and supinator muscle groups of the upper limb and the flexor and abductor muscles of the lower limb. This pattern of weakness is sometimes referred to as a 'pyramidal distribution'.

In lower motor neurone lesions, weakness may affect individual muscles or groups of muscles. The pattern of weakness is determined by the site of the lesion. Anterior horn cell disease initially causes a focal weakness but may eventually become generalized. Nerve root lesions result in weakness in the myotome innervated by the spinal segment that corresponds to the involved root. Similarly, plexus lesions cause weakness in the myotomes that correspond to the involved roots. Peripheral nerve lesions cause weakness in the muscles that are innervated by the affected nerve.

Table 2.22
Summary of clinical features of patients presenting with weakness.

Site of lesion	Inspection	Tone	Power	Tendon reflexes	Plantar response
Upper motor neurone	No wasting	Increased	Pyramidal pattern of weakness	Increased	Extensor
Lower motor neurone	Wasting Fasciculations	Decreased	Weakness in affected muscles	Decreased	Flexor
Neuromuscular junction	Wasting uncommon	Usually normal; may be decreased	Fatigable weakness Bilateral	Usually normal	Flexor
Muscle	May have wasting	Decreased	Predominantly proximal limb girdle Bilateral	Decreased	Flexor
Non-organic weakness	Normal	Normal	Predominantly proximal limb girdle Erratic, give-away weakness	Normal	Flexor

Neuromuscular junction disease, such as myasthenia gravis, characteristically causes fatigability of muscle strength. The weakness predominantly affects the proximal muscles of the limb girdles, although the ocular, bulbar and respiratory muscles are also often involved.

Myopathy generally causes bilateral and proximal weakness of the limb muscles. However, the muscles of the face, neck and trunk may also be involved.

Reflexes

There are two kinds of reflexes that need to be tested:

(a)   tendon reflexes; and
(b)   cutaneous reflexes.

Tendon reflexes

Tendon reflexes test stretch reflex contraction, which is brought about by striking a muscle tendon with a patellar hammer. These reflexes may be heightened or diminished; if tendon reflexes are absent, they can sometimes be elicited using reinforcement. For upper limb reflexes, reinforcement involves asking the patient to clench the jaw at the same time as the reflex is tested for. For lower limb reflexes, the same is achieved by asking the patient to pull the hands apart with the fingers interlocked. Tendon reflexes are graded using the notation in *Table 2.23*.

Table 2.23
Grading of tendon reflexes.

Tendon reflex	Grade
Very brisk	+++
Brisk	++
Normal	+
Absent	0
Present with reinforcement	±
Clonus	CL

The tendon reflexes that should routinely be examined include the biceps reflex, the supinator reflex, the triceps reflex, the knee reflex and the ankle reflex. *Fig. 2.13* shows how to examine these reflexes and their respective root values. Brisk reflexes or clonus are signs of an upper motor neurone lesion above the root level of the reflex. Diminished or absent reflexes are signs of lower motor neurone lesion or muscle disease.

Cutaneous reflexes

The cutaneous reflexes that are routinely tested in clinical practice include the plantar response and the superficial abdominal reflex.

To elicit the plantar response, the skin of the lateral border of the foot is stroked firmly using an orange stick. A flexor plantar response, in which all the toes flex, is normal. An extensor plantar response, in which the big toe extends while the other toes spread out, indicates an upper motor neurone lesion. Occasionally there is no response; this may occur with upper motor neurone weakness or with a sensory abnormality over the foot.

To elicit an abdominal reflex, the skin of each abdominal quadrant is stroked swiftly, horizontally across, using an orange stick. Normally, the abdominal wall on the same side contracts. Note that the skin above the umbilicus is innervated by the thoracic root T8–T9 and the skin below the umbilicus by thoracic root T10–T11, and that therefore the abdominal reflex is absent in pyramidal lesions above these root levels. It is also absent in some cases of obesity and in patients with a history of abdominal operations.

Co-ordination and cerebellar function

Smooth and accurate movement requires the successful integration of sensory feedback and motor output. This is carried out principally by the cerebellum, which receives sensory inputs detailing the position of the body and its limbs. Therefore, the clinical tests of co-ordination, which test cerebellar function and detect lesions of the cerebellum (see *Table 2.24*), should be interpreted with caution when there is a loss of joint position sense or when there is also muscle weakness.

Finger–nose test and heel–shin test
In the finger–nose test, the patient is asked to touch the examiner's index finger, held at an arm's length from the patient, with the tip of his or her own index finger and then to touch the end of his or her nose. This is repeated several times without stopping. The test can be made more sensitive by moving the target finger.

The heel–shin test is a similar test to the finger–nose test but using the legs. The patient is asked to place the heel of one foot on the knee of the other leg and slide the heel down along the shin and then to lift it clear and repeat this action.

The finger–nose test and the heel–shin test detect intention tremor and dysmetria. An intention tremor is absent at rest but develops as the patient moves willfully. Dysmetria is the inability to perform accurate targeted movements. Instead, movements are jerky and the target is overshot ('past pointing').

Repetitive movements
The patient is asked to slap the palm and then the back of the hand alternately on his or her own knee. This is then repeated as rapidly as possible. Alternatively, the patient is asked to tap the floor rapidly with the toes of one foot.

A patient with dysdiadochokinesia is unable to perform such rapid alternating movements and instead moves irregularly, loses the pattern and uses uneven force.

Other tests and signs of cerebellar function
The remaining tests of cerebellar function are discussed in the relevant sections. The signs

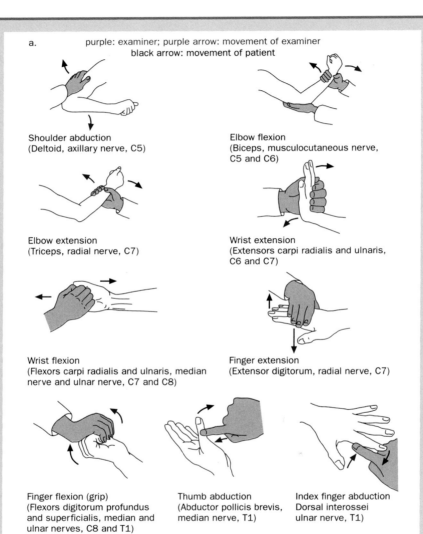

a.   purple: examiner; purple arrow: movement of examiner
black arrow: movement of patient

Shoulder abduction
(Deltoid, axillary nerve, C5)

Elbow flexion
(Biceps, musculocutaneous nerve,
C5 and C6)

Elbow extension
(Triceps, radial nerve, C7)

Wrist extension
(Extensors carpi radialis and ulnaris,
C6 and C7)

Wrist flexion
(Flexors carpi radialis and ulnaris, median
nerve and ulnar nerve, C7 and C8)

Finger extension
(Extensor digitorum, radial nerve, C7)

Finger flexion (grip)
(Flexors digitorum profundus
and superficialis, median and
ulnar nerves, C8 and T1)

Thumb abduction
(Abductor pollicis brevis,
median nerve, T1)

Index finger abduction
Dorsal interossei
ulnar nerve, T1)

Figure 2.12
Testing the power of muscles groups of the (a) the upper limb and (b) the lower limb.

b.   purple: examiner; purple arrow: movement of examiner
black arrow: movement of patient

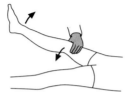

Hip flexion
(Iliopsoas, lumbar plexus
and femoral nerve, L1 and L2)

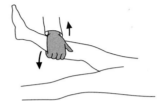

Hip extension
(Gluteus maximus, inferior
glutial nerve, L5 and S1)

Knee flexion
(Hamstrings, sciatic
nerve, S1 and S2)

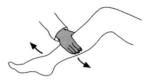

Knee extension
(Quadriceps femoris,
femoral nerve, L3 and L4)

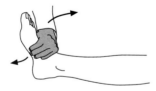

Ankle dorsiflexion
(Tibialis anterior,
deep peroneal nerve,
L4 and L5)

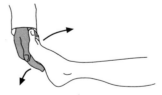

Ankle plantar flexion
(Gastrocnemius and soleus,
sciatic nerve, S1 and S2)

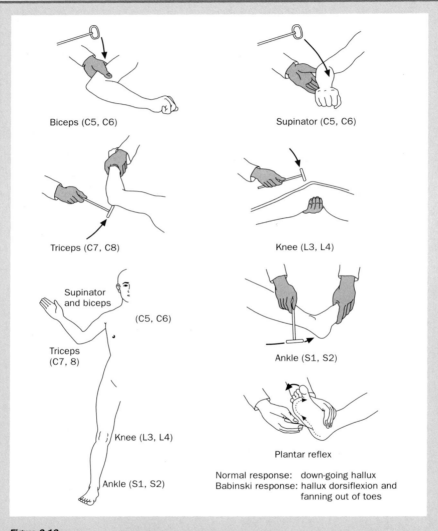

Figure 2.13
Eliciting tendon and cutaneous reflexes.

Table 2.24
Causes of cerebellar lesions.

> *Multiple sclerosis*
> *Stroke*
> *Tumour*
>   *Secondary (e.g. from lung, breast, cutaneous melanoma)*
>   *Primary (e.g. from medulloblastoma, astrocytoma)*
>   *Non-metastatic manifestations*
> *Toxins (e.g. alcohol)*
> *Drugs (e.g. phenytoin)*
> *Infections (e.g. abscess)*
> *Metabolic (e.g. myxoedema)*
> *Inherited cerebellar ataxias (e.g Friedreich's ataxia)*

that are elicited are summarized here for convenience.

• Truncal ataxia

When asked to sit up from a lying position without the use of the hands, the patient falls to one side.

• Ataxic dysarthria

The speech is slow, slurred and scanning. Words are often broken down into their component syllables and uttered with varying force.

• Eye signs

Pursuit movements are slow and feature 'catch-up' saccadic movements that attempt to maintain target fixation. Eye movements also exhibit hypometric saccades or hypermetric saccades, in which the eyes undershoot or overshoot the target when fixating. Cerebellar lesions also produce horizontal nystagmus in which the fast phase points towards the side of the lesion.

• Hypotonia

Hypotonia is a minor feature of cerebellar dysfunction.

• Pendular tendon reflexes

• Ataxic gait

The ataxic gait is broad-based, unco-ordinated and unsteady, with the patient veering towards the side of the lesion.

Extrapyramidal features

In a routine neurological examination, the extrapyramidal features that are sought include:

(a) on inspection: abnormal movements and poverty of movement;

(b) when testing tone: lead-pipe or cogwheel rigidity; and

(c) when examining gait: a Parkinsonian gait.

However, if an extrapyramidal syndrome is suspected, several other specific features are sought; these are discussed in Chapter 5.

Sensory system

Anatomy

There are two main pathways that relay sensory information:

(a) the dorsal (posterior) columns; and

(b) the spinothalamic tracts.

The dorsal (posterior) columns carry sensory information concerning light touch, vibration and proprioception (*Fig. 2.14*). The spinothalamic tracts carry information concerning pain and temperature (see *Fig. 2.14*).

Sensory innervation is much more variable than motor innervation, and the usual sensory dermatomes and cutaneous distribution of nerves are illustrated in *Fig. 2.15*.

Examination

There are five basic modalities of sensation:

(a) light touch;

(b) pain;

(c) vibration;

(d) proprioception; and

(e) temperature.

These can be tested using the following methods.

Light touch

The patient, with eyes closed, is gently touched on the skin with a piece of cotton wool and asked to respond 'yes' to acknowledge each contact. Note that it is important that the skin is touched and that the cotton wool is not dragged, since this will stimulate other receptors.

Pain

With the patient's eyes closed, a sharp or blunt stimulus is randomly applied to the skin and the patient is asked to identify the nature of the stimulus on each occasion.

Vibration

With the patient's eyes closed, the stem of a 128 Hz tuning fork is placed on a bony prominence and the patient is asked if the vibration can be felt. Testing is carried out from distal to proximal points. In the lower limbs, begin with the big toe and move proximally to the metatarsophalangeal joint, then to the ankle and knee and finally to the anterior superior iliac spine. In the upper limbs, begin by testing a finger tip and then move proximally to the metacarpophalangeal joint, wrist and elbow and finally to the shoulder. If vibration is absent on testing the limbs, move on to the sternum and the chin. Note that if the sense of vibration is found to be normal at distal sites then more proximal testing is not necessary.

Proprioception

With the patient's eyes closed, proprioception is tested by moving a joint through successively smaller angles and asking the patient the extent and direction of motion. Begin distally and move proximally if necessary.

Temperature

As a screening test, it is adequate to touch the skin with a tuning fork and ask whether the patient feels it as cold. For more formal testing, tubes filled with cold or hot water are used.

Specialized tests

Two-point discrimination

With the patient's eyes shut, the skin is touched with either one or both prongs of a blunted pair of compasses and the patient is asked to state how many points can be felt. The distance between the prongs is gradually reduced and the distance at which the patient can no longer distinguish two points is noted. Normally, two points can be distinguished at a distance of 5 mm on the index finger and 7 mm on the little finger.

Test for sensory inattention

The patient is asked to identify when the right side of the body is touched, then the left side and then both sides. Normally, all are identified correctly. However, with sensory inattention the patient acknowledges correctly when touched on either side but only identifies one side when both are stimulated together.

Test for astereognosis

Astereognosis is the inability to recognize objects by form and texture. The patient is

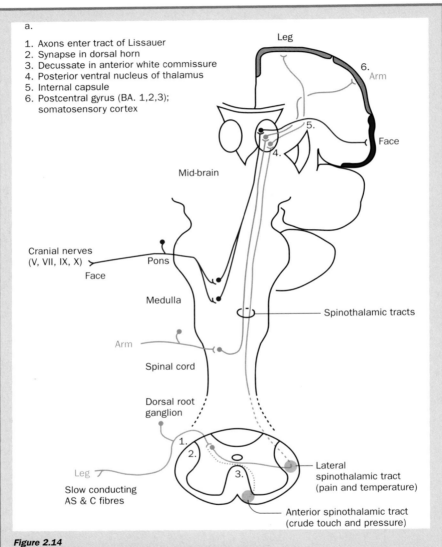

a.

1. Axons enter tract of Lissauer
2. Synapse in dorsal horn
3. Decussate in anterior white commissure
4. Posterior ventral nucleus of thalamus
5. Internal capsule
6. Postcentral gyrus (BA. 1,2,3); somatosensory cortex

Leg

6.
Arm

5.

4.

Face

Mid-brain

Cranial nerves
(V, VII, IX, X)
Face

Pons

Medulla

Spinothalamic tracts

Arm

Spinal cord

Dorsal root
ganglion

1.

2.

3.

Leg

Slow conducting
AS & C fibres

Lateral
spinothalamic tract
(pain and temperature)

Anterior spinothalamic tract
(crude touch and pressure)

Figure 2.14
(a) The spinothalamic system and (b) the dorsal column system.

b.

1. Vibration and touch
2. Contribution to dorsal horn pain-gating neurones
3. Afferent component of monosynaptic reflexes
4. Posterior ventral nucleus of the thalamus
5. Internal capsule
6. Somatosensory cortex

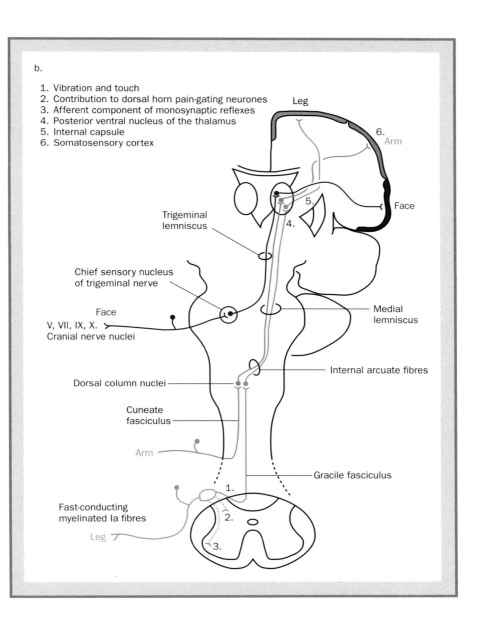

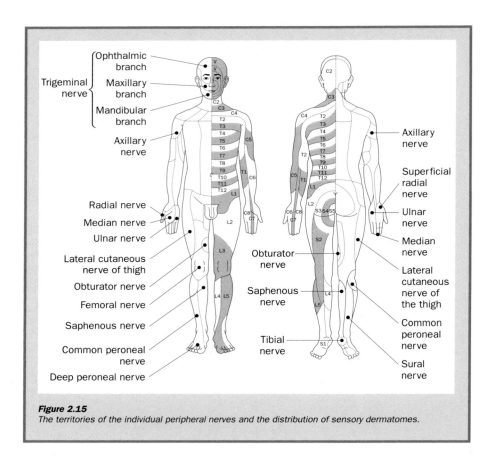

Figure 2.15
The territories of the individual peripheral nerves and the distribution of sensory dermatomes.

asked to identify objects such as a coin by touch alone with the eyes closed.

Test for agraphaesthesia
Agraphaesthesia is the inability to recognize figures drawn on the palm of the hand. The patient is asked to identify numbers drawn on the palm of a hand with his or her eyes closed.

Interpretation of tests

The pattern of sensory loss depends on the site of the lesion.

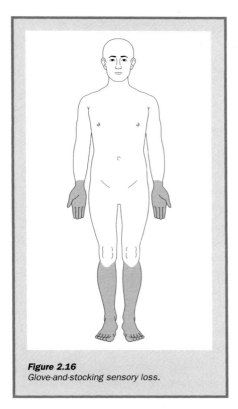

Figure 2.16
Glove-and-stocking sensory loss.

Nerve lesions
• Peripheral nerves
Lesions of peripheral nerves produce sensory loss in a glove-and-stocking distribution (*Fig. 2.16*).

• Single nerve
In lesions of a single nerve, sensory loss occurs in the cutaneous distribution of the nerve (*see Fig. 2.15*).

• Root
In nerve root lesions, sensory loss occurs in the distribution of the root or of several roots (see *Fig. 2.15*).

Spinal cord lesions
• Complete transverse section of the spinal cord
A complete transverse section of the spinal cord leads to a loss of all modalities below the level of the lesion.

• Hemisection of the spinal cord (Brown–Sequard syndrome)
Hemisection of the spinal cord leads to ipsilateral loss of proprioception and vibration and contralateral loss of pain and temperature below the level of the lesion.

• Lesion of the central part of the spinal cord
A lesion of the central part of the spinal cord leads to loss of pain and temperature at the level of the lesion, where the spinothalamic fibres cross, but other modalities remain intact. This is referred to as dissociated sensory loss.

• Dorsal column lesion
A dorsal column lesion leads to loss of proprioception and vibration with preserved pain, light touch and temperature sensation.

- Anterior spinal syndrome

In anterior spinal syndrome there is loss of pain, temperature and light touch sensation with preserved proprioception and vibration.

Brainstem lesions

Brainstem lesions cause loss of pain and temperature on the ipsilateral side of the face and the contralateral side of the body.

Thalamic lesions

Lesions in the thalamus cause hemisensory loss of all modalities.

Parietal lobe lesions

In parietal lobe lesions all sensation modalities are recognized but localization is poor, with sensory inattention, astereognosis and the loss of two-point discrimination.

Gait

Examination

The patient is requested to walk barefoot as per normal and then to walk heel-to-toe. Observe and note:

(a)   the posture;

(b)   the separation between the feet;

(c)   the size of each step;

(d)   the height to which the knees are lifted;

(e)   the manner in which the legs are swung;

(f)   the movements of the pelvis and shoulders;

(g)   the extent of arm swing; and

(h)   the overall symmetry of the gait.

Patterns of gait abnormalities

Parkinsonian gait

The patient maintains a stooped posture and has difficulty starting, stopping and turning around. Steps are typically small, slow and shuffling. There is a tendency to fall forward and therefore successive steps are taken with increasing speed so as to catch up (festination). The arm swing is noticeably poor.

Cerebellar gait

The patient walks with the feet spaced widely apart. The gait is unco-ordinated (ataxic) and unsteady and the patient veers towards the side of the cerebellar lesion. In mild cases, the ataxic gait may only be present on walking heel-to-toe in a straight line.

Apraxic gait

An apraxic gait is usually the consequence of frontal lobe lesions. Initiating walking is difficult and the patient walks with feet spaced widely apart and by taking small steps. However, there may be no abnormality of power, sensation or co-ordination.

Hemiparetic gait

The patient has a characteristic hemiparetic posture with flexion of the upper limb and extension of the lower limb. The affected leg appears stiff and is swung out in a semicircle (circumduction), enabling the foot to clear the floor.

Spastic gait

The legs are adducted at the hips such that they may cross over (scissoring) when the patient walks. Movement is slow and stiff.

Steppage gait

This occurs with foot drop, in which the patient is unable to dorsiflex the ankle. When the patient walks the knee is lifted high so that the foot clears the floor; when the leg is lowered the foot makes a slapping sound on the floor.

Myopathic gait

This occurs with proximal muscle weakness of the lower limb girdle. Characteristically, it is a waddling gait in which the body's weight is alternately placed on each leg, with the opposite hip and side of the trunk tilting up towards the weight-bearing side. However, the weak gluteal muscles cannot stabilize the weight-bearing hip, which sways outward, and so the opposite pelvis drops, as does the trunk on that side.

Sensory ataxia

This arises as a result of impaired proprioception. The patient is unsteady and walks with the feet wide apart, lifting them high off the ground and stamping on the floor. In addition, Romberg's test (see below) is positive.

Antalgic gait

This arises from lower limb or pelvic pain on walking. The patient tends to bear weight mainly on the unaffected side, only briefly putting weight on the affected side.

Functional gait

This is a bizarre gait, which is inconsistent or worsens when being observed. A psychogenic cause must be considered.

Romberg's test

In Romberg's test, the patient is initially asked to stand with the feet together and the eyes open. The eyes are then closed. Observe whether the patient remains steady (and be prepared to intervene and support the patient in case of a fall).

If the patient is steady with the eyes open but begins to fall when the eyes are closed, this is termed 'Romberg's-test positive' and indicates a loss of proprioception. Swaying backwards and forwards upon eye closure suggests a cerebellar syndrome. Severe unsteadiness with eyes open and feet together is indicative of cerebellar or vestibular syndromes.

Investigations

3

On the basis of a history and examination, a hypothesis is formed as to the cause of the patient's clinical symptoms. Often investigations are necessary to reach a definitive diagnosis; therefore, at this stage, these investigations are planned carefully and carried out systematically. The aim of the investigations is to define a lesion in terms of its location and pathophysiology. The types of investigations that are used range from simple laboratory tests to complex clinical procedures and sophisticated neuroimaging techniques. Investigations should be chosen on the basis of whether they are likely to provide useful diagnostic and clinical information.

Examination of the cerebrospinal fluid
Lumbar puncture (spinal tap)

A lumbar puncture involves the insertion of a needle into the subarachnoid space for diagnostic, therapeutic or anaesthetic purposes. The patient lies in the left lateral position; the back is perpendicular to the bed and the spine is maximally flexed by pulling the knees up to the chest. A vertical line through the iliac crests identifies the lumbar L3–L4 space. In a sterile environment, the skin and subcutaneous tissues are anaesthetized and the lumbar puncture needle is introduced, usually in the L3–L4 or the L4–L5 space, angled towards the patient's umbilicus. Note that the introduction of the needle into the subarachnoid space can usually be felt by a 'give' in the resistance of the tissue to the advance of the needle. The stylet within the needle is then withdrawn. The cerebrospinal fluid (CSF) pressure is measured using a manometer and some CSF is collected in three sterile bottles, and a fluoride tube to determine the glucose level. (The indications, contraindications and complications of lumbar puncture are listed in *Tables 3.1–3.3*.) Note that concurrent blood tests for glucose and oligoclonal bands are performed for comparison with the CSF findings.

CSF tests

The CSF can be analysed for the following parameters (normal values are shown in *Table 3.4*):

(a) cells, protein and glucose (CSF glucose is compared with serum glucose);
(b) microbiological studies (Gram stain and culture); Ziehl–Nielsen stain and culture for tuberculosis; serological tests for syphilis; viral and fungal studies;
(c) cytology for malignant cells; and

(d) electrophoresis looking for oligoclonal bands as an indication of multiple sclerosis.

Clinical neurophysiology
Electroencephalography

Electroencephalography (EEG) involves recording the spontaneous electrical activity of the brain using surface electrodes applied to the scalp. The electrodes are attached at standardized positions, and the small electrical signals that are detected are amplified, displayed and recorded. An eight- or sixteen-channel tracing is usually used to map the electrical activity of the brain when the patient is awake or asleep, and the signal can be modified or enhanced by active hyperventilation, sleep deprivation or photic stimulation.

In specialist centres, EEG recordings can be made on ambulant patients in conjunction with simultaneous video recording in order to correlate clinical events with electrical changes. This is known as videotelemetry.

Interpretation of an EEG record requires considerable experience, and the normal EEG wave forms are distinguished by their morphology, frequency, location and reactivity. *Table 3.5* describes the features of normal EEG wave forms. *Table 3.6* summarizes some abnormal EEG patterns and their possible aetiology.

Table 3.1
Indications for lumbar puncture.

Diagnostic indications
    Central nervous system infections
    Subarachnoid haemorrhage
    Demyelinating disorders (e.g. multiple sclerosis)
    Other inflammatory disorders (e.g. sarcoidosis, Guillain–Barré syndrome)
    Vasculitis
    Unexplained dementia with progressive course and acute onset
    Idiopathic intracranial hypertension (in order to measure opening pressure)
    Normal-pressure hydrocephalus (in order to predict response to shunt)
    Myelography (in order to introduce contrast medium)
Therapeutic indications
    Intrathecal administration of medications (e.g. chemotherapy)
    Removal of CSF in idiopathic intracranial hypertension
    Blood patch for treatment of post-lumbar puncture headaches
Anaesthetic indications
    Epidural block for pain management or during labour

Table 3.2
Contraindications to performing a lumbar puncture.

Suspected or actual raised intracranial pressure (risk of coning) except in idiopathic
    intracranial hypertension
Local lumbar sepsis
Bleeding disorder or anticoagulation therapy
Significant spinal deformity

Table 3.3
Complications of lumbar puncture.

Iatrogenic post-lumbar puncture meningitis
Post-lumbar puncture headache
Bleeding (e.g. spinal, epidural, subdural, subarachnoid)
Transient unilateral abducens nerve palsy
Backache
Occasional transient lower limb paraesthesia
Brain herniation

Table 3.4
Normal CSF findings.

Clear, colourless fluid	
Pressure	80–180 mmH$_2$O
Cells	0–5 lymphocytes/mm^3
Protein	0.2–0.5 g/l
Glucose	2.5–4.4 mmol/l (>60% of blood glucose)

Table 3.5
Normal EEG wave forms.

Rhythm	Frequency (Hz)	Features
Alpha	8–13	Symmetrical, parieto-occipital region
		Enhanced by eye closure; disappears with eye opening
Beta	>13	Symmetrical, frontal
		Unaffected by eye opening
Theta	4–8	Frontal and temporal predominance
		Occurs normally during sleep, abnormally during wakefulness
Delta	<4	Frontal and temporal predominance
		Occurs normally during deep sleep, abnormally during wakefulness

In clinical practice, the EEG is used mainly in:

(a) epilepsy;
(b) encephalitis; and
(c) coma.

In epilepsy, an EEG is sometimes helpful in localizing the origin of the epilepsy and describing seizure types. It can usually differentiate epilepsy from non-epileptic events; however, it is important to note that the EEG can be normal in epileptic patients. EEG sensitivity can be enhanced by using provocative procedures such as active hyperventilation, sleep deprivation or photic stimulation; in patients with suspected psychogenic seizures (pseudoepilepsy), the more reliable method of EEG telemetry (prolonged video and EEG monitoring; videotelemetry) can be used.

Table 3.6
Abnormal EEG patterns.

Pattern of activity	Cause
Generalized slow wave (theta or delta waves) activity	Diffuse cerebral disease (e.g. inflammatory or metabolic encephalopathy)
Focal slow wave activity	Underlying focal structural lesion
Focal or generalized spikes, or spike and slow wave activity	Epilepsy
3 Hz bilateral, symmetrical spike-and-wave activity	Typical absence seizure
Generalized multiple spike-and-wave activity	Myoclonic epilepsy
Periodic, generalized 1–2 Hz sharp waves over low amplitude and slow background	Creutzfeldt–Jakob disease

Table 3.7
Characteristic EEG wave-form patterns in encephalitis.

Herpes simplex encephalitis is indicated by periodic lateralized epileptiform discharges
Subacute sclerosing panencephalitis is indicated by repetitive slow wave discharges alternating with periods of relative electrical silence
Creutzfeldt–Jakob disease is suggested by periodic, generalized 1–2 Hz sharp waves over low amplitude and slow background

EEG is also used before a surgical intervention in epilepsy to help localize the epileptic focus. Depth electrodes, which are inserted directly into the brain, are positioned at sites determined clinically and by surface EEG recordings. Surgery that is confined to patients whose depth recordings confirm surface EEG findings has a much better outcome.

In encephalitis, some abnormal EEG wave-form patterns points to specific aetiologies (*Table 3.7*).

In coma, EEG is useful for providing both diagnostic and prognostic information.

Evoked potentials

Evoked potentials (EPs) are used to assess the integrity of sensory pathways. A sensory nerve is repeatedly stimulated, and the responses are recorded through surface electrodes placed on the cerebral cortex or the spine, or both. A computer then averages the responses after removing background noise.

The EPs in common clinical use are as follows:

• Visual EPs

Recording electrodes are placed over the occipital region, and a unilateral retina is stimulated by having the patient look at a moving black-and-white chequer board. An abnormality suggests a lesion along the visual pathway.

Visual EPs are useful for assessing patients who are suspected of having multiple sclerosis and functional visual loss.

• Brainstem auditory EPs

The unilateral auditory nerve is stimulated by a constant clicking sound while the other ear is masked. The electrical activity is recorded from the lateral surface of the scalp. The resulting evoked response consists of a series of components, each of which arises from activity in different segments of the auditory pathway.

Brainstem auditory EPs are useful for assessing patients who are suspected of having brainstem lesions, including multiple sclerosis, posterior fossa tumours and acoustic neuroma. They are also used to evaluate patients who have prolonged periods of depressed consciousness and for screening hearing in normal children or in those who have suffered meningitis.

• Somatosensory EPs

The recording electrodes are placed over the spine and somatosensory cortex, and the peripheral nerves of the arms and legs are stimulated electrically.

Somatosensory EPs are useful for assessing patients who are suspected of having multiple sclerosis or functional hemisensory loss.

Electromyography and nerve conduction studies

Needle electromyography and nerve conduction studies are usually performed together.

Electromyography

In electromyography, a needle electrode is inserted into a muscle and impulses are measured with the muscle at rest or during voluntary contraction. The morphology, amplitude, duration, number of phases and complexity of the wave form are then assessed.

Normally, muscles at rest are electrically silent unless the needle is placed in the region of the motor end-plate (in which case miniature end-plate potentials are recorded). In abnormal muscles, spontaneous activity can be seen at rest. The abnormal activities at rest include fibrillations, fasciculations and positive sharp waves.

Fibrillations and positive sharp waves are due to spontaneous contractions of individual muscle fibres; they cannot be observed through the skin. They commonly occur in muscle diseases but may occur in some neurological disorders. Fasciculations represent the contractions of groups of muscle fibres that are supplied by a motor unit; they are seen as a ripple through the skin. They occur in muscle denervation after damage to peripheral nerves, nerve roots or anterior horn cells.

Motor unit potentials, which are produced by a group of muscle fibres that are supplied by a motor neurone, are evaluated during minimal voluntary contraction and are used to differentiate neuropathic and myopathic disorders.

Nerve conduction studies

Nerve conduction studies evaluate two aspects:

(a) motor nerve conduction; and
(b) sensory nerve conduction.

In motor nerve conduction studies, an accessible motor nerve is stimulated by a surface electrode or a needle electrode, usually at two different sites, and the compound motor action potential is recorded using an electrode placed over an innervated muscle. In sensory nerve conduction studies, a sensory nerve is stimulated, and the sensory action potential is recorded using an electrode placed over the appropriate nerve trunk proximal to the stimulated site. The following parameters are measured:

(a) latency; the time required for nerve stimulation to produce a motor or sensory action potential;
(b) amplitude; the height of the action potential;
(c) the morphology;
(d) conduction velocity; the calculated velocity between the stimulated sites.

As a general rule, demyelination is suggested by a reduction in conduction velocity, whereas axonal loss is suggested by a reduction in amplitude. Electromyographic and nerve conduction studies are used to determine:

(a) the cause of a particular weakness (e.g. anterior horn cell disease, radiculopathy, plexopathy, neuropathy, neuromuscular junction disorder or myopathy) or sensory abnormalities;
(b) the distribution of an abnormality (e.g. focal or generalized); and

(c) the type of neuropathy (e.g. axonal or demyelinating; motor, sensory or sensorimotor) or myopathy (e.g. myositis or dystrophy).

Other techniques

Repetitive nerve stimulation

In repetitive nerve stimulation, a motor nerve is subjected to repetitive stimulation, and the resulting compound motor action potential is measured. It is a technique that is used to detect neuromuscular junction disorders. Normally, the action potential has a constant amplitude; however, in myasthenia gravis the action potential rapidly fatigues, as evidenced by a decrement in amplitude. Interestingly, presynaptic disorders, specifically the Lambert–Eaton myasthenic syndrome, may be associated with an incremental response to repetitive stimulation.

Single-fibre electromyography

In single-fibre electromyography, fine needle electrodes are inserted into a pair of muscle fibres that are innervated via one anterior horn cell, and recordings are made during minimal voluntary contraction. Normally, the pair of muscle fibres fire synchronously, but in neuromuscular junction disorders they fire irregularly (known as 'jitter').

Transcranial magnetic stimulation

In transcranial magnetic stimulation, the motor cortex is stimulated by application of a magnetic pulse, and the motor response is recorded in a distal muscle in the contralateral limb. This enables the central motor conduction time to be assessed.

Tissue biopsies

Brain biopsy

A brain biopsy is considered when all other investigations have failed to provide a diagnosis and when the diagnosis may influence the treatment and prognosis. The biopsy is performed when the site of the lesion can be localized, the lesion is accessible and a critical region such as the brainstem is not involved. Most brain biopsies are performed by stereotactic techniques. Complications include haemorrhage, infection and neurological deficit.

A brain biopsy is indicated in:

(a) suspected primary brain tumours or single metastases;

(b) infections (e.g herpes simplex encephalitis); and

(c) progressive, degenerative disorders.

Nerve biopsy

A nerve biopsy is indicated in unexplained peripheral neuropathy when all diagnostic tests have been exhausted. It is commonly performed under local anaesthetic from the sural nerve behind the lateral malleolus, which leaves no motor deficit and only a small patch of sensory loss.

Muscle biopsy

A muscle biopsy is undertaken routinely in most patients who are suspected of having primary muscle disease. The biopsy is performed under local anaesthetic using an incision or needle. The sample is taken from a weak muscle that has not previously been subjected to electromyographic needling. The procedure carries a minimal risk of infection.

Temporal artery biopsy

A temporal artery biopsy is performed in suspected cases of temporal arteritis

Neuroimaging
Plain X-rays

Plain X-rays of the skull and spine are useful in the initial evaluation of patients who have suffered acute trauma in order to exclude fractures. Although largely superseded by computed tomography, X-rays of the spine are nevertheless useful in the routine assessment of back pain.

Computed tomographic scans

Computed tomographic (CT) images are dependent on the attenuation (i.e. the loss of energy and slowing) of X-ray photons as they pass through tissues of varying density. Those X-ray photons that emerge are detected and recorded using scintillation counters, and, from these data, computer images are mathematically reconstructed and displayed as radiodensity maps. Further enhancement can be achieved by administering iodinated contrast agents, which highlight areas of increased vascularity (e.g. tumours and vascular malformations) and regions where there is a breach of the blood–brain barrier.

CT is superior to magnetic resonance imaging for detecting intracerebral haemorrhage (particularly subarachnoid haemorrhage) and calcified lesions. However, CT is less sensitive and specific than magnetic resonance imaging for detecting most other cranial and spinal pathology. Note that high-density matter, such as bone, appears white on CT and that low-density matter, such as CSF, appears black (*Fig. 3.1*).

Magnetic resonance imaging

Magnetic resonance imaging (MRI) exploits the behaviour of protons when they are

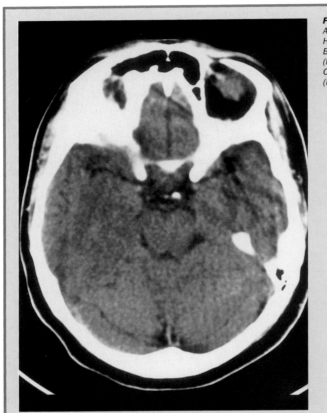

Figure 3.1
A CT scan.
Horizontal section.
Bone appears white
(high-density matter).
CSF appears black
(low-density matter).

subjected to a strong magnetic field. The application of such a field aligns the atomic spin axes and produces precession, in which the axial rotation of each atom is specific. The subsequent delivery of a radiofrequency impulse that imparts energy promotes a transient shift of some nuclei to a higher quantum level; this is called 'resonance'. The subsequent return of the nuclei, called 'relaxation', results in the emission of radiofrequency waves, which are then detected as the magnetic resonance signal. The rate of alignment of displaced protons, along with other features such as the proton density, gives

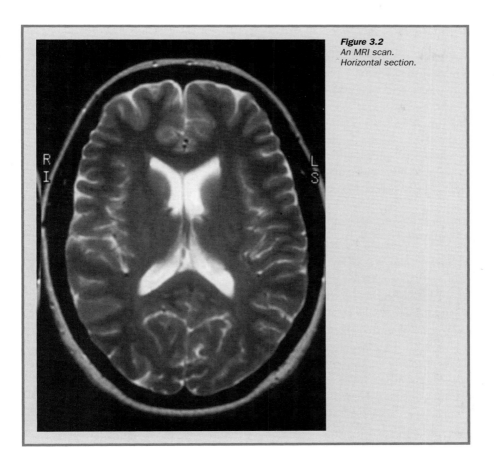

Figure 3.2
An MRI scan.
Horizontal section.

information about the physical properties of the tissue, and it is this that is reconstructed using a computer to provide images in any plane. Additional refinement is provided by the use of intravenous contrast agents (such as gadolinium) to enhance lesions or to detect disruption to the blood–brain barrier.

MRI is more sensitive and specific than CT for detecting brain and spinal cord lesions, since it provides higher resolution (*Fig. 3.2*). However, MRI is expensive and is contraindicated in patients with metallic implants.

Myelography

Myelography is useful for imaging the spinal cord and nerve roots. It involves injecting a water-soluble contrast agent into the subarachnoid space via a lumbar puncture, and then taking X-rays of the relevant section of the spine. The flow of contrast along the spinal canal is controlled by using a tilt table. However, since the advent of spinal MRI, myelography is now rarely used.

Cerebral angiography and spinal angiography

These are invasive procedures that are used to view cranial or spinal blood vessels. A contrast agent is injected via a catheter that has been inserted into the femoral or brachial artery and threaded through to the vessel to be examined. A series of X-rays are taken while the contrast agent outlines the branches of the carotid and vertebral arteries and then the capillary and venous beds.

Indications for cerebral or spinal angiography include:

(a) cases in which CT or MRI have failed to provide definite answers;

(b) cases in which a vascular lesion is suspected (e.g. vasculitis or arteriovenous malformations);

(c) suspected arterial dissection;

(d) cases in which carotid endarterectomy is being contemplated; and

(e) the obliteration of arteriovenous malformation by the injection of particles.

Angiography is associated with a 1% morbidity and mortality.

Digital subtraction angiography

In digital subtraction angiography, the contrast agent is injected intravenously, and computed subtraction of the precontrast image from the postcontrast image allows display of the vessels. DSA is adequate for studying extracranial arteries but not intracranial arteries.

Magnetic resonance angiography

Magnetic resonance angiography (MRA) is a non-invasive technique that delineates blood vessels using magnetic resonance. It is made possible because blood vessels produce a low signal. However, MRA is not as sensitive as conventional angiography, but is a useful alternative for patients who are allergic to contrast agents or for elderly patients and patients with renal failure. Furthermore, with rapid improvements in technology, MRA is often sufficient in cases where conventional angiography would previously have been necessary.

CT angiography

High-resolution CT scanning with intravenous contrast and subtraction techniques (CT angiography) can also be used to visualize blood vessels.

Carotid Doppler ultrasonography

Carotid Doppler ultrasonography is a non-invasive method that detects the velocity of blood flow and determines the degree of carotid artery stenosis. It is widely used, particularly in patients with transient ischaemic attacks or those who have suffered a stroke.

Functional imaging techniques

Most of the techniques that have been described above provide mainly structural information about the central nervous system. In addition to these techniques, there are several techniques that primarily image brain function. Although most of these are currently research tools, they will no doubt have wider clinical use in the near future. These functional imaging techniques are listed in *Table 3.8.*

Table 3.8
Functional imaging techniques.

Positron emission tomography (PET)
Single photon emission computed tomography (SPECT)
Functional magnetic resonance imaging (fMRI)
Magnetic encephalography (MEG)
Magnetic resonance spectroscopy (MRS)

Headaches

4

Headache is one of the most common reasons for medical consultation. This is especially the case in neurological and psychiatric settings.

Pathophysiology

The brain parenchyma is insensitive to pain. The cranial structures that are sensitive to pain include:

(a) blood vessels—intracranial arteries, extracranial arteries, and intracranial venous sinuses and their tributaries;
(b) parts of the dura mater;
(c) cutaneous and subcutaneous structures, skeletal muscle, and the periosteum of the skull; and
(d) the eyes, ears, teeth, nasal cavities and sinuses.

Intracranial lesions cause headaches only if they impinge on one of these structures. The pain of intracranial disease is mainly conveyed by the trigeminal nerve, but the facial, glossopharyngeal and vagus nerves and the upper three cervical roots also transmit pain sensation. Generally speaking, pain from the supratentorial structures is referred to the anterior two-thirds of the head via branches of the trigeminal nerve, whereas pain from the infratentorial structures is referred to the vertex and the back of the head and neck by the upper cervical roots.

Types of headache

Headaches can be divided broadly into two categories:

(a) primary headaches, in which there is no obvious underlying organic cause; and
(b) secondary headaches, which are symptomatic of an underlying condition.

Table 4.1 gives a classification of headaches.

Primary headache disorders

Migraine

Migraine is a recurrent, episodic headache associated with abnormal sensory sensitization (e.g. to light, sounds, smell or movement).

Epidemiology

Migraine is a common cause of headache. The overall 1-year prevalence is about 10% and the lifetime prevalence is about 15%, although these figures vary widely in different studies. Women are affected more often than men, with female to male ratios of between 2:1 and 3:1. The peak incidence is in the second and third decades. Migraine may start in childhood, but onset after 50 years of age is unusual. There is a family history of migraine in up to 85% of patients.

Clinical features

A migraine attack can be divided into four phases, although not all phases always occur.

• Prodome (premonitory phase)
This phase occurs hours to days before the headache, and most patients describe characteristic features, which may be:

(a) psychological (e.g. depression, irritability, euphoria);
(b) neurological (e.g. dysphasia, yawning, hyperosmia);
(c) constitutional (e.g. sluggishness, anorexia, hunger); or
(d) autonomic (e.g. urination, diarrhoea, constipation).

Some patients describe a vague feeling that a migraine attack is imminent.

• Aura
The aura is a complex of focal neurological symptoms that precedes or accompanies the headache. It is characterized by:

(a) visual phenomena (e.g. spots, flashing lights, zigzag lines);

Table 4.1
Primary and secondary headaches.

> **Primary headache disorders**
> Migraine
> Tension-type headache
> Cluster headache and chronic paroxysmal headache
>
> **Secondary headache disorders**
> Head trauma
> Vascular disorders
> Non-vascular intracranial disorders
>   Cerebrospinal fluid pressure disorders
>   Intracranial space-occupying lesion
>   Intracranial infection
>   Inflammatory disorders
> Substances or their withdrawal
> Non-cephalic infection
> Metabolic disorders
> Headache or facial pain associated with disorder of cranium, neck, eyes, ears, nose,
>   sinuses, teeth, mouth or other facial or cranial structures
> Cranial neuralgias, nerve trunk pain and deafferentation pain
> Unclassifiable headache
>
> *Adapted from the formal classification proposed by the International Headache Society.*

(b) sensory phenomena (e.g. tingling, paraesthesia, numbness—usually starting in the limbs and face); or

(c) motor phenomena (e.g. limb weakness, dysphasia).

The aura usually lasts less than 1 hour.

• Headache
The headache in migraine is usually unilateral, throbbing, of moderate to severe intensity and aggravated by movement. It is invariably associated with nausea and vomiting, photophobia (sensitivity to light), phonophobia (sensitivity to sound) and osmophobia (sensitivity to smell). It usually lasts between 4 and 72 hours. Note that it can also be bilateral.

• Resolution phase
Following the headache the patient may have mood changes, impaired concentration,

lethargy and scalp tenderness for a variable period of time.

Several migraine syndromes are recognized, of which migraine with aura (classical migraine) and migraine without aura (common migraine) are the most common. Some of these syndromes are described below.

• Migraine with aura (classical migraine)
As the name implies, the aura precedes or accompanies the headache in this type of migraine attack.

• Migraine without aura (common migraine)
The headache is similar to that of migraine with aura except that the aura is absent.

• Basilar migraine
This is migraine with an aura that is clinically localized to the brainstem or to both occipital lobes. The aura can be characterized by visual symptoms in both the temporal and nasal fields of both eyes, dysarthria, vertigo, tinnitus, decreased hearing, diplopia, ataxia, bilateral paraesthesia, bilateral pareses or a decreased level of consciousness.

• Hemiplegic migraine
Migraine associated with hemiparesis can occur as a sporadic or familial disorder. Weakness may last for hours or days or even, in rare cases, for weeks. Recovery is usual, except in the rare situation in which cerebral infarction occurs.

• Ophthalmoplegic migraine
Usually, in this rare syndrome, an oculomotor palsy occurs in association with the headache. Trochlear and abducens nerve involvement have also been described. The ophthalmoplegia can last for days or weeks, and sometimes residual dysfunction can occur.

Most patients recognize some triggers that precipitate migraine attacks. The common precipitants are listed in *Table 4.2*.

Diagnosis

In most patients, the diagnosis is established almost exclusively by taking a detailed history. Neurological examination is usually normal, except during an attack of hemiplegic or

Table 4.2
Triggers of migraine headaches.

Stress
Physical exertion
Missed sleep
Travel
Bright lights
Diet
Certain foods (e.g. chocolate, cheese)
Alcohol
Missed meals
Hormonal factors
Oral contraceptive agents
Premenstrual or menstrual timing
Release from stress

Table 4.3
Drugs used in the treatments of migraines.

Acute attack treatments	Prophylactic treatments
Aspirin	Pizotifen
Paracetamol	β-Blockers
Non-steroidal anti-inflammatory drugs	Propranolol
Ibuprofen	Metoprolol
Naproxen	Tricyclic antidepressants
Tolfenamic acid	Amitriptyline
Triptans	Dothiepin
Sumatriptan	Imipramine
Naratriptan	Sodium valproate
Rizatriptan	Methysergide
Zolmitriptan	
Ergotamine	

ophthalmoplegic migraine, or in migraine complicated by cerebral infarction.

Management

General measures
The patient should be advised to avoid clear-cut triggers and to adopt regular habits. Regular sleep, exercise, meals, work habits and relaxation may result in a reduction in the frequency of migraines.

Drug therapy
Remedies for acute attacks are divided into:

(a) non-disease-specific medications (e.g. analgesics and non-steroidal anti-inflammatory drugs); and

(b) disease-specific treatments (e.g. the triptans and ergotamine derivatives).

Most medications for acute attacks (especially those that contain opiates) have a propensity to aggravate headache frequency and induce chronic daily headaches. For this reason, the use of these drugs should be limited. Coadministration of an antiemetic medication can be useful when nausea and vomiting are prominent symptoms. For frequent attacks, regular daily treatment with prophylactic agents may be necessary.

Table 4.3 lists the drugs that are used in an acute migraine attack and those that are used for prophylaxis.

Tension-type headache

Epidemiology

Tension-type headache is the most common headache, with a lifetime prevalence of about 70%. As with migraine, the condition is more common in women than in men.

Clinical features

This headache is bilateral. The pain is non-throbbing and described as a pressure sensation or tightness around the top of the head ('an iron band'). It is usually a featureless headache—that is to say, it is not exacerbated by movement and there is no nausea, vomiting, photophobia, phonophobia or osmophobia. However, occasionally, either photophobia or phonophobia may be present. The pain is usually mild to moderate and does not limit daily activities. Most patients have episodic headaches that last between 30 minutes and several days, although some have the chronic variety. Tension headaches may be associated with anxiety, depression or stress.

Neurological examination is invariably normal, although some patients may have scalp tenderness as a result of chronic pericranial muscle contraction.

Management

The management of tension-type headaches is divided into psychological, physiological and pharmacological treatment.

- Psychological treatment
Psychological therapies or a referral to a psychiatrist are used to deal with emotional issues or if the patient shows signs of serious mental disturbance.

- Physiological treatment
Physiological treatments, in the form of relaxation therapy or biofeedback, are used to promote relaxation, especially of the overcontracted pericranial muscles.

- Pharmacological treatment
Pharmacotherapy is used in conjunction with psychophysiological treatments. Amitriptyline is the drug of choice, since it appears to confer benefit irrespective of the presence or absence of depression. Simple analgesics can stop or reduce the severity of an individual attack; however, repeated use can lead to rebound headaches as the analgesia wears off and, therefore, their use should be limited.

Cluster headache

Epidemiology

Cluster headache is a rare condition with a prevalence of 0.1%. It affects men more frequently than women, in a ratio of between 3:1 and 9:1. The incidence rate is highest from the second to the fourth decade.

Clinical features

Cluster headache is a strictly unilateral headache, although it may switch sides from one attack to the next. The pain is usually orbital or periorbital but it can be present anywhere in the affected half of the head. The headache is very severe, with the pain lasting from 15 minutes to 3 hours. The pain is accompanied by various ipsilateral autonomic features including conjunctival injection, lacrimation, eyelid oedema, ptosis, miosis (partial Horner's syndrome), nasal blockage and rhinorrhoea. Patients tend to move around or rock with the pain. Patients can have up to eight attacks per day, and the attacks often occur at particular hours of the day or night, characteristically waking the patient from sleep.

Cluster headaches are described as being either episodic or chronic. In the episodic form, the attacks occur in bouts over periods of 2–3 months, interspersed with periods during which the patient is completely free from attacks. In the chronic form, attacks of pain occur over periods of more than 1 year with no remission being longer than a fortnight.

Diagnosis

In most patients, the diagnosis is established on the basis of the clinical features, and investigations are unnecessary.

Management

The management of cluster headache is divided into treatment of an acute attack and preventive treatment.

Acute attacks can be treated with 100% oxygen at the flow rate of 10–12 l/minute inhaled for 15 minutes, 6 mg of sumatriptan subcutaneously or 4% lignocaine intranasally.

The options available for preventive treatment depend on whether the patient has episodic or chronic cluster headaches. These options are summarized in the *Table 4.4.*

Secondary headaches

Only the more common or important causes of symptomatic headaches are discussed here.

Headache due to head trauma

A post-traumatic headache begins within 2 weeks of the injury or of regaining consciousness. It may cease after a short period of time or persist for a very prolonged period of time.

Headache due to vascular disorders

Numerous vascular disorders are associated with headaches, including:

(a) acute ischaemic cerebrovascular disease—transient ischaemic attacks or thromboembolic stroke;

Table 4.4
Preventive treatments for cluster headaches.

Episodic cluster headaches	Chronic headaches
Prednisolone	Verapamil
Verapamil	Lithium
Methysergide	Methysergide
Ergotamine (taken daily at night)	Valproate
Valproate	

(b) intracranial haemorrhage—intracerebral, subdural or extradural haemorrhage;

(c) subarachnoid haemorrhage;

(d) vascular malformation—aneurysm or arteriovenous malformation;

(e) venous thrombosis; and

(f) acute arterial hypertension (e.g. phaeochromocytoma, malignant hypertension).

Headache due to subarachnoid haemorrhage

Subarachnoid haemorrhage is caused by spontaneous bleeding into the subarachnoid space.

Epidemiology
The incidence rate is 10–15 cases per 100,000 of the population per year.

Aetiology
The causes of subarachnoid haemorrhage are summarized in *Table 4.5.*

Clinical features
The patient is struck down by a severe headache of sudden onset, often described as

Table 4.5
The causes of subarachnoid haemorrhage.

Common causes
Rupture of a saccular (berry) aneurysm (70%)
Arteriovenous malformations (5%)

Rare causes
Coagulopathies
Tumour
Vasculitis
Use of oral contraceptive pill

Cause unknown (20%)

'like being struck on the back of the head by a sledge hammer'. The headache is associated with nausea, vomiting and photophobia. There may be an initial, transient or prolonged alteration of consciousness.

Neurological examination reveals signs of meningism:

(a) neck stiffness on passive flexion; and
(b) positive Kernig's sign (with the patient lying supine, flexing the leg at the hip with the knee flexed and then trying to extend the knee causes pain and is resisted).

Papilloedema may be present and may be accompanied by subhyaloid and vitreous haemorrhage. Focal signs, determined by the location of the haematoma, may develop.

Investigations

CT scanning is the initial investigation of choice in suspected subarachnoid haemorrhage. It detects subarachnoid or intraventricular blood in 90% of patients when the scan is performed within 24 hours of onset.

Lumbar puncture is performed if the CT scan is normal or not available. Analysis of the cerebrospinal fluid shows xanthochromia (straw-coloured supernatant, caused by red blood cell haemolysis) from 12 hours to up to 1 week.

Angiography is performed to localize aneurysms and arteriovenous malformations.

Management

The immediate management of subarachnoid haemorrhage involves:

(a) resuscitation;
(b) analgesia for the headache;
(c) administration of nimodipine (a calcium channel blocker) to reduce vasospasm;
(d) control of hypertension; and
(e) transfer to a neurosurgical unit.

Subsequently, an angiogram is carried out to localize the cause and to plan any surgical intervention.

Prognosis

Approximately 45% of patients die within the first 3 months. The risk of rebleeding within the first month is approximately 30% and is maximal in the first 2 weeks. For long-term survivors, the risk of bleeding is 3% per year.

Subdural haemorrhage

Aetiology

A subdural haemorrhage occurs as a result of bleeding into the subdural space from ruptured bridging veins between the cortex and venous sinuses. It is almost invariably caused by trauma to the head. The predisposing factors, besides head injury, are old age (cortical atrophy stretches the bridging veins), alcoholism, epilepsy and anticoagulant use.

Clinical features

A subdural haemorrhage may present in two different ways—acute or chronic. In acute subdural haemorrhage, there is rapid accumulation of blood, which leads to a space-occupying effect including transtentorial coning. The patient presents soon after the head injury with a rapid decline in the level of consciousness and focal neurological signs. In chronic subdural haemorrhage, the initial injury has usually been mild and there is a latent period of days to months from injury to presentation. Headache is the most frequent symptom, often accompanied by a fluctuating level of consciousness and focal neurological deficits.

Management
Imaging by CT or MRI scanning will usually show the haemorrhage. The haematomas are drained either via burr holes or by craniotomy.

Extradural haermorrhage

Aetiology
An extradural haemorrhage is caused by a traumatic tear in the middle meningeal artery, usually associated with a lateral skull fracture.

Clinical features
The patient presents with headache, vomiting, focal neurological signs and declining level of consciousness, often after a period of lucidity.

Management
The management is the same as for a subdural haemorrhage.

Headaches due to non-vascular intracranial disorders

Non-vascular intracranial disorders that can cause headache include cerebrospinal fluid pressure disorders, intracranial tumours, intracranial infection and inflammatory conditions.

Raised intracranial pressure

The causes of raised intracranial pressure (ICP) are listed in *Table 4.6.*

Clinical features
Since the skull is not compressible, raised ICP, regardless of the underlying cause, produces a unique pathophysiological process with characteristic symptoms and signs.

The cardinal symptom is a generalized headache, which is worse in the morning and gradually regresses as the day goes on. The headache worsens with actions that further increase the ICP, such as coughing, straining and changes in posture. Nausea and vomiting

Table 4.6
Causes of raised intracranial pressure.

Primary
Idiopathic intracranial hypertension (benign intracranial hypertension)

Secondary
Hydrocephalus
Mass lesion
 Tumour
 Abscess
 Haemorrhage
Meningitis or encephalitis
Trauma
Major intracranial and extracranial venous obstruction
Drugs
 Vitamin A, tetracycline, nitrofurantoin, oral contraceptive pill, anabolic steroids, steroid withdrawal
Systemic disease
 Renal disease, systemic lupus erythematosus

---

are associated with the headache, as are impaired visual acuity and visual obscurations (transient loss of vision). With a serious rise in ICP, the patient may develop impairment of consciousness.

Neurological examination reveals papilloedema, although it may be absent even in the presence of a large intracranial mass. There may be focal signs relating to the site of the mass lesion, along with false localizing signs such as abducens nerve palsy. The patient may also develop bradycardia and hypertension.

Investigations

Imaging of the brain with CT or MRI is essential. A lumbar puncture is contraindicated because of the risk of coning, except in idiopathic intracranial hypertension (see below).

Idiopathic intracranial hypertension (benign intracranial hypertension)

Epidemiology

The incidence of benign intracranial hypertension is 1 case per 100,000 of the

Table 4.7
The causes of low CSF pressure.

Spontaneous (no evidence of CSF leak or systemic illness)
Symptomatic (associated with CSF leak or systemic illness)
  After lumbar puncture
  Head or back trauma
  Postoperative
    Craniotomy or spinal surgery
  Spontaneous CSF leak
  Systemic illness
    Dehydration, diabetic coma, uraemia

population per year. It predominates in young, overweight women in whom the incidence rate is much higher.

Clinical features

Patients present with headaches, nausea, vomiting and visual symptoms including blurred vision, transient obscurations (typically triggered by postural changes) and diplopia (secondary to abducens nerve palsy).

Neurological examination reveals papilloedema and various visual field defects, including an enlarged blind spot, central scotoma and constriction of peripheral vision. Abducens nerve palsy may also be present.

Investigations

CT or MRI scans are usually normal, although the lateral ventricles may appear small. Lumbar puncture confirms raised CSF pressure, but CSF composition is normal.

Management

Weight loss is advised if the patient is overweight. Acetazolamide, which is thought to have an inhibitory effect on the production of CSF, and corticosteroids can also be used. Repeated lumbar punctures are often performed to relieve the pressure.

However, surgical intervention may eventually be necessary, either to drain the CSF via a lumboperitoneal shunt or to protect the optic nerve via optic nerve sheath incisions. (This allows the optic nerve subarachnoid space to communicate with the orbital contents.)

Low ICP

Aetiology

The causes of low ICP are listed in *Table 4.7*.

Clinical features

Almost all patients with symptomatic intracranial hypotension have headache. The headache may be frontal, occipital or generalized. It is aggravated by an upright position and relieved by lying down (orthostatic headache). It is also aggravated by head-shaking, coughing, straining, sneezing and jugular compression. Associated symptoms include nausea, vomiting, tinnitus, photophobia, anorexia and general malaise.

Physical examination is usually normal, although there may be mild neck stiffness and bradycardia ('vagus pulse').

Investigations

Gadolinium-enhanced MRI shows diffuse meningeal enhancement in most patients. CSF pressure is usually low, ranging from 0 to 70 mmH$_2$O. However, CSF composition is normal.

Intracranial space-occupying lesions

Space-occupying lesions, such as tumours and abscesses, cause a headache only when they impinge on the pain-sensitive structures. Thus, it is the site rather than the size of the lesion that determines the onset of headache, and infiltrating lesions may become quite extensive before they cause a headache. These lesions present with features of raised intracranial pressure, focal neurological features or diffuse cerebral symptoms, such as seizures and cognitive impairment.

Infection

Meningitis and encephalitis are associated with headaches.

Meningitis

Meningitis is an inflammatory reaction of the meninges.

Aetiology

Inflammation of the meninges can be caused by:

(a) infectious agents;
(b) chemical agents (e.g. drugs, contrast media; blood after a subarachnoid haermorrhage); and
(c) tumour infiltration.

However, only infectious meningitis is discussed further here.

Infectious meningitis can be caused by bacteria, viruses or fungi (*Table 4.8*). The most likely causative organisms vary with age and predisposing factors (*Table 4.9*).

Clinical features

There may be a prodrome with myalgia and lethargy in association with a likely source of infection, such as pneumonia or otitis media.

Table 4.8
Causes of infectious meningitis.

Bacteria
Neisseria meningitidis (meningococcus)
*Streptococcus pneumoniae
(pneumococcus)*
Haemophilus influenzae
Listeria monocytogenes
Escherichia coli
*Staphylococcus aureus, Staphylococcus
epidermidis*
Mycobacterium tuberculosis
Spirochaetes
   Treponema pallidum (syphilis)
   Borrelia burgdorferi (Lyme disease)

Viruses
Enteroviruses
   Echovirus
   Coxsackie virus
   Poliovirus
Mumps virus
Herpes simplex virus, herpes zoster virus
Epstein–Barr virus
Human immunodeficiency virus (HIV)

Fungi
Cryptococcus neoformans
Candida spp.
Histoplasma capsulatum

The patient then rapidly (within minutes to hours) develops a severe headache, which is associated with pain and stiffness in the neck and back, photophobia and vomiting. Some patients may even present with an altered level of consciousness or seizures.

Examination reveals fever with rigors,

although this is variable, and signs of meningism (neck stiffness on passive flexion and a positive Kernig's sign). The appearance of impaired consciousness, papilloedema, cranial nerve lesions, focal neurological deficits and seizures indicates complications such as venous sinus thrombosis, severe cerebral oedema, hydrocephalus, subdural empyema or cerebral abscess. Septic shock with disseminated intravascular coagulation can also develop.

The specific varieties of meningitis are discussed below.

• Bacterial meningitis
Bacterial meningitis is characterized by the sudden onset of a high fever and rigors. A non-blanding petechial rash indicates meningococcal meningitis. Occasionally, patients present with septic shock.

• Viral meningitis
Viral meningitis is usually a benign, self-limiting illness manifesting as meningism without prominent systemic symptoms or focal signs. Recovery occurs over 7–14 days, although the headache may persist for some weeks.

• Tuberculous meningitis
Tuberculous meningitis is typically chronic, commencing with a vague headache, malaise, anorexia and vomiting. Meningitic signs may take weeks to appear, but impaired

Table 4.9
The most likely causative organisms of infectious meningitis according to age and predisposing factors.

Neonates
   Gram-negative bacilli (e.g. *Escherichia coli*)
   β-haemolytic streptococci
Children
   Neisseria meningitidis
   Streptococcus pneumoniae
   Haemophilus influenzae
Adults
   Neisseria meningitidis
   Streptococcus pneumoniae
Immunocompromised patients
   Gram-negative organisms
   Listeria monocytogenes
   Cryptococcus neoformans
   Mycobacterium tuberculosis
Head trauma and neurosurgical patients (including patients with an intracranial shunt or
   reservoir)
   Gram-negative bacilli
   Staphylococcus aureus, Staphylococcus epidermidis

consciousness, focal neurological signs and seizures can occur.

• Fungal meningitis
Cryptococcal meningitis is the most common fungal meningitis in Europe. It presents as a chronic illness that is similar to tuberculous meningitis.

Investigations
Diagnosis is made by lumbar puncture. If there is no suggestion of raised intracranial pressure, an immediate lumbar puncture should be performed. The CSF findings are summarized in *Table 4.10*. CSF should be stained (Gram stain for bacteria, Ziehl–Nielsen stain for *Mycobacterium tuberculosis* and Indian-ink stain for fungi) and cultured (including culture in Lowenstein–Jensen medium for *Mycobacterium tuberculosis*). Serological tests for viruses and syphilis also need to be requested.

In patients with signs of papilloedema, an altered level of consciousness or focal neurological deficit, a CT scan is mandatory before a lumbar puncture is performed.

A complete infection screen and chest and

Table 4.10
CSF findings in meningitis.

	Normal	Bacterial meningitis	Viral meningitis	Tuberculous meningitis
Appearance	Clear	Turbid or purulent	Clear or turbid	Turbid or viscous
Neutrophils	Nil	200–10000/mm³	Nil or few	0–200/mm³
Lymphocytes	<5 per mm³	<50 per mm³	10–100 per mm³	0–200 per mm³
Protein	0.2–0.4 g/l	0.5–2.0 g/l	0.4–0.8 g/l	0.5–3.0 g/l
Glucose	More than half the blood glucose level	Less than half the blood glucose level	More than half the blood glucose level	Less than half the blood glucose level

skull (sinus) X-rays are necessary in order to exclude a primary source of infection.

Management

• Bacterial meningitis

Bacterial meningitis can lead to death in a matter of hours, and therefore early diagnosis and appropriate antibiotic treatment are essential. It is usually possible to distinguish bacterial meningitis from meningitis caused by other organisms on the basis of clinical findings and CSF examination. The choice of an appropriate antibiotic is crucial and is dependent on the age of the patient, the clinical symptoms and signs and whether an organism has been isolated. The options are:

(a) before the organism has been identified:
  (i) for neonates cefotaxime and ampicillin;
  (ii) for children and adults, cefotaxime or benzylpenicillin (chloramphenicol if allergic to penicillins);
(b) after the organism has been identified:
  (i) for meningococcal or pneumococcal meningitis, benzylpenicillin (chloramphenicol if allergic to penicillins);
  (ii) for meningitis caused by *Haemophilus* spp. or *Escherichia coli*, cefotaxime.

The use of corticosteroids remains controversial, the main indications being children infected with *Haemophilus* spp. and adults with rapidly declining neurological function.

• Tuberculous meningitis

Tuberculous meningitis is treated with a combination of isoniazid (with pyridoxine to prevent peripheral nerve side effects), rifampicin and pyrazinamide for 9 months. Other possible agents include ethambutol, streptomycin and ciprofloxacin.

• Viral meningitis

Viral meningitis, as stated above, is usually benign and self-limiting, and the treatment is therefore symptomatic.

Prophylaxis

Contacts of patients with bacterial meningitis should be considered for prophylactic treatment with rifampicin.

Inflammatory disorders

Inflammatory disorders such as temporal arteritis, sarcoidosis and systemic lupus erythematosus can cause headaches.

Temporal arteritis (giant cell arteritis)

Pathology

Granulomatous inflammatory changes (with giant cells) occur in medium-sized and large arteries. The blood vessels show narrowing of the lumen and may become occluded with thrombus.

Epidemiology

Temporal ateritis is rare in patients who are under the age of 50 years. The incidence increases dramatically after the age of 50 years, when it occurs in 3–9 per 100,000 per year, and it is an important condition to exclude in an elderly patient who presents with a new-onset headache. Women are affected three times more often than men.

Clinical features

Patients usually present with headaches, which often localize to the temples but may be generalized. The pain can be intermittent or constant and is exacerbated by contact (e.g. brushing the hair or wearing a hat). It is associated with scalp tenderness, especially over the inflamed superficial temporal arteries. Patients may complain of pain on chewing (jaw claudication), which occurs because of impaired blood supply to the muscles of mastication.

Many patients may have constitutional symptoms, including malaise, anorexia, weight loss, night sweats and low-grade fever. Polymyalgia rheumatica (which is characterized by stiffness and pain in the shoulder and pelvic girdle muscles as well as constitutional upset) may antedate the headache or coincide with it.

Visual loss, which occurs as a result of occlusion of ciliary and retinal arteries, is the most feared complication of temporal arteritis. Transient loss of vision in one eye (amaurosis fugax) may occur before persistent visual loss. Diplopia may occur as a result of oculomotor or abducens palsy.

Neurological examination may reveal tender, thickened and non-pulsatile superficial temporal arteries. Rarely, scalp necrosis may occur. Fundoscopy may show a swollen optic disc, which later becomes pale. There may be evidence of other rare complications, including brainstem ischaemia, cortical blindness, cranial nerve lesions, aortitis and involvement of the coronary and mesenteric arteries.

Investigations

The erythrocyte sedimentation rate (ESR) is substantially raised, although rarely it is normal. Serum alkaline phosphatase levels may be raised. A positive result from a superficial temporal artery biopsy confirms the diagnosis, but a negative result does not exclude it since the artery may not be uniformly affected along its length ('skip lesions').

Management

Patients are treated urgently with corticosteroid therapy after a blood sample has been taken for ESR but before a superficial temporal artery biopsy is performed. The dose is gradually reduced, titrating it against the patient's symptoms and ESR. Treatment is usually necessary for 12–24 months.

Table 4.11
Medications that can induce headaches.

Antihypertensive agents	Calcium channel blockers, angiotensin converting enzyme inhibitors
Vasodilators	Glycerine trinitrate
Antidepressants	SSRIs, moclobemide, monoamine oxidase inhibitors venlafaxie, refuzodone
Antipsychotics	Phenothiazines, atypical neuroleptics
Antibiotics	Tetracyclines, trimethoprim
Cholesterol-lowering agents	Gemfibrozil, bezafibrate, simvastatin
Ulcer-healing drugs	Ranitidine, cimetidine

Headaches associated with drugs

Numerous drugs can induce headaches *Table 4.11*. The sudden withdrawal of drugs, such as caffeine, SSRIs and ergot derivatives, can also induce headaches.

Patients who have frequent headaches (e.g. chronic tension-type headache and frequent migraine) often overuse analgesics, ergot derivatives and triptans. Medication overuse by headache-prone patients frequently produces both drug-induced rebound headache and dependence on the medications. This results in a chronic daily headache. Furthermore, medication overuse can make the headaches refractory to preventive medications. Thus, patients who are prone to frequent headaches should be encouraged to limit the use of analgesic medications. Those who have developed a chronic daily headache should be encouraged to stop the symptomatic medications. This initially results in withdrawal symptoms with increased headache frequency, but the headache subsequently improves. Thereafter, preventive medications can be initiated if necessary.

Headaches caused by disorders of the cranial and facial structures

Disorders of the various cranial and facial structures can cause pain (*Fig. 4.1*).

Cranial neuralgias

Trigeminal neuralgia (tic douloureux)

Epidemiology
Trigeminal neuralgia has a prevalence of 15 cases per 100,000. The male-to-female ratio is 3:2. The onset of the condition usually occurs after the age of 40 years, with a mean age of onset of about 50 years.

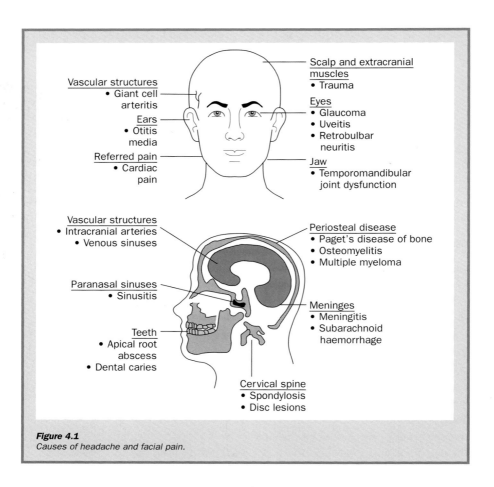

Figure 4.1
Causes of headache and facial pain.

Aetiology

The causes include:

(a) idiopathic trigeminal neuralgia (caused by vascular compression);

(b) multiple sclerosis;

(c) intracranial aneurysms; and

(d) intracranial tumour.

The idiopathic form is thought to be triggered

by the cross-compression of the trigeminal nerve by blood vessels.

Clinical features

Trigeminal neuralgia is characterized by paroxysms of jabs or stabs of intense pain, lasting seconds, in the distribution of one or more of the branches of trigeminal nerves. The mandibular and maxillary divisions are more frequently affected than the ophthalmic division. The pain is usually unilateral, with only 4% of patients reporting bilateral paroxysms.

The pain may be provoked by stimulation of specific trigger points, or by cold, washing, shaving, chewing, talking or brushing the teeth. The pain may precipitate hemifacial muscle spasms (hence the term 'tic douloureux').

Typically, remission occurs and lasts for months or years, but in a few the pain may become chronic.

Physical examination is normal except for the trigger points. Impaired sensation in the trigeminal nerve distribution suggests a demyelinating or structural lesion.

Investigations

MRI scanning is performed to exclude structural lesions.

Management

The drug of choice is carbamazepine. Phenytoin and baclofen are less effective than carbamazepine, and are therefore used when carbamazepine is ineffective or not tolerated. Invasive treatments include:

(a) alcohol block of the peripheral branch of the painful division of the trigeminal nerve;

(b) percutaneous radiofrequency thermocoagulation of the trigeminal nerve sensory root; and

(c) microvascular decompression of the trigeminal nerve (performed via an occipital craniotomy and involving the removal of any aberrant blood vessels that are compressing the nerve).

Post-herpetic neuralgia

Patients who have suffered shingles (herpes zoster virus reactivation) in the branches of the trigeminal nerve may suffer persistent pain in the affected region after the rash has healed. The pain of post-herpetic neuralgia has three components:

(a) constant, deep, burning pain;

(b) repetitive stabbing sensations; and

(c) superficial, sharp pain or itching provoked by light touch.

The pain can last for 2–3 years after the eruption. It is treated with tricyclic antidepressants or topical application of capsaicin.

Clinical approach to headaches

History and examination

A detailed history is essential for diagnosis, and the approach to the management is dependent on the nature of onset of the headache and its subsequent course. Although the clinical examination is usually entirely normal, any abnormalities must not be overlooked since they will guide subsequent diagnostic and treatment strategies. *Table 4.12* summarizes the important aspects of history and examination.

Differential diagnosis

The differential diagnosis depends on the pattern of the headache. *Table 4.13* gives common differential diagnosis by mode of onset.

Investigations

A careful history and physical examination are sufficient to make the diagnosis in the vast majority of patients with headaches.

Blood tests

Routine blood tests have a role in excluding symptomatic causes of headache and should be performed when there are symptoms or signs of systemic disorder, infection or meningeal reaction. An ESR is essential in a patient over the age 55 years who presents with headache, to rule out temporal arteritis.

Neuroimaging

CT and MRI

Routine neuroimaging has a low likelihood of uncovering significant intracranial disease in patients with headache who have a normal physical and neurological examination. CT or MRI scanning are indicated in some specific instances (*Table 4.14*). Gadolinium-enhanced MRI scans are very useful in patients who are suspected of having a low CSF pressure (see page 77).

Cerebral angiography

Cerebral angiography is indicated in cases in which an aneurysm, an arteriovenous malformation or vasculitis is suspected.

Lumbar puncture

A lumbar puncture is essential in the following clinical situations, preferably after a CT or MRI scan:

(a) rapid or recent onset of a severe headache;

(b) severe, rapid-onset, recurrent headaches;

(c) a progressive headache; and

(d) atypical chronic intractable headache.

Table 4.12
History and examination of the patient who presents with headache.

> ### History
> Detailed description of headaches
>   Nature of attack onset—acute, subacute or chronic
>   Site, radiation and laterality of pain
>   Character of pain
>   Frequency and duration
>   Associated features—other neurological symptoms, neck stiffness, autonomic
>   symptoms
>   Exacerbating factors—movement, light, noise, smell, coughing, sneezing, bending
>   Precipitating factors—diet, alcohol, menstruation, stress, postural change, head injury
>   Ameliorating factors
> Past headache history
> Systems review
>   Existing medical conditions
> Family history
>   Migraine, hypertension, intracranial haemorrhage and other neurological disorders
> Drug history
>   Analgesic abuse, recreational drugs
> Social history
>   Impact of headache
>
> ### Examination
> General examination
>   Signs of systemic disease
> Cardiovascular system
>   Blood pressure
> Neurological system
>   Fundoscopy—papilloedema
>   Signs of meningism—neck stiffness and Kernig's sign
>   A full neurological examination is essential to exclude a focal neurological deficit
> Head and neck
>   Signs of local disease of the ears, eyes and sinuses
>   Restriction of neck movements and neck pain
>   Temporomandibular dysfunction
>   Thickening of the superficial temporal arteries

Table 4.13
Differential diagnosis of headache according to its mode of onset.

Acute onset of severe headache
Subarachnoid haemorrhage
Intracerebral haemorrhage
Meningitis and encephalitis
Acute hydrocephalus
Acute hypertension (e.g. phaeochromocytoma)
First episode of cluster headache or crash migraine

Subacute-onset headache
Subdural or extradural haematoma
Intracranial tumour
Intracranial abscess
Chronic meningitis
Temporal arteritis
Idiopathic intracranial hypertension

Chronic daily headache
Chronic migraine with or without analgesic overuse
Chronic tension-type headache with or without analgesic overuse
Post-herpetic neuralgia
Post-traumatic headache

Recurrent episodic headache
Migraine
Cluster headache
Trigeminal neuralgia
Intermittent hydrocephalus
Paroxysmal hypertension

Table 4.14
Situations in which CT or MRI scanning is indicated in the investigation of headache.

Rapid or recent onset of a severe headache
Change in the frequency, severity or clinical features of headache attacks
Progressively worsening headache
Headache associated with:
    abnormal neurological examination
    seizures
    personality changes
    systemic ill-health

A lumbar puncture is indicated when the clinical suspicion of subarachnoid haemorrhage is high but neuroimaging of the brain is normal. It is also indicated for the diagnosis of meningitis or encephalitis and for the measurement of CSF pressure, especially in idiopathic intracranial hypertension.

Movement disorders

5

Movement disorders can be broadly divided into two categories:

(a) akinetic–rigid syndromes, which are characterized by diminished movement and muscular rigidity; and
(b) dyskinesias, which are characterized by abnormal, involuntary movements.

Akinetic–rigid syndromes

The akinetic–rigid syndromes are often referred to as the Parkinsonian syndromes. They are listed in *Table 5.1*.

Idiopathic Parkinson's disease

Epidemiology

Idiopathic Parkinson's disease is the most common movement disorder. Its prevalence in the UK is about 100 per 100,000 of the population, rising to about 500 per 100,000 for those over the age of 50 years. Both sexes are equally affected and it occurs in all races, but it appears to be more common in Europe and North America.

Table 5.1
Akinetic–rigid syndromes.

Idiopathic Parkinson's disease
Secondary Parkinsonism (Parkinson-plus syndromes)
    Caused by other neurodegenerative disorders
        Multiple system atrophy
        Progressive supranuclear palsy
        Corticobasal degeneration
        Diffuse Lewy body disease
    Caused by other definable causes
        Drugs (e.g. dopamine receptor antagonists, lithium, α-methyldopa)
        Toxins (e.g. manganese, carbon monoxide poisoning)
        Vascular disorders (e.g. atherosclerosis)
        Postencephalitic disorders (e.g. encephalitis lethargica)
        Head injury, including punch-drunk syndrome
        Brain tumour
        Hydrocephalus, high-pressure and hydrocephalus and normal-pressure hydrocephalus
        Metabolic disorders (e.g. Wilson's disease)

Pathology

The main pathological finding in Parkinson's disease is the progressive degeneration of cells within the pars compacta of the substantia nigra. Macroscopically, this is recognized by the loss of the characteristic melanin pigmentation of this region. Microscopically, the surviving neurones in the affected areas often contain eosinophilic inclusions known as Lewy bodies.

The substantia nigra projects to the striatum (the caudate nucleus, putamen and related structures) via the nigrostriatal pathway, which utilizes dopamine as its neurotransmitter. Striatal dopamine deficiency is thus the cardinal biochemical feature of Parkinson's disease, leading to an abnormality in the normal neurotransmitter balance in favour of cholinergic and other transmitter mechanisms.

Aetiology

The aetiology of Parkinson's disease remains unknown. Discordance in twin studies suggests that genetic factors do not play a significant role, and therefore environmental agents may be responsible for the disease. Support for an environmental basis came from the finding that drug addicts who take heroin that is contaminated with 1-methyl-4-phenyl-1,2,3,6-tetrahydropyridine (MPTP) develop a similar condition to Parkinson's disease, with selective destruction of the nigral cells and their striatal connections. However, no consistent environmental factor has been definitely identified, although there have been tentative suggestions that Parkinson's disease is weakly associated with exposure to pesticides and wood pulp.

Clinical features

Parkinson's disease is characterized by a clinical triad of tremor, rigidity and bradykinesia (slowness of movement), in association with abnormalities of posture and gait. Onset of the disease is typically asymmetrical, so much so that a symmetrical onset casts doubt over the diagnosis of idiopathic Parkinson's disease.

Tremor

A tremor is the initial complaint in about two-thirds of those with Parkinson's disease, and it occurs eventually in most patients. It is most common in the upper and lower limbs but occasionally involves the head (titubation), jaw, lips, tongue or trunk. In the hands it is often described as 'pill rolling'—a combination of flexion and extension of the fingers with a pronator–supinator movement at the forearm. A typical Parkinsonian tremor, with a frequency of 4–6 Hz, is present at rest and is intensified by mental or emotional stress and diminished by purposeful movements or sleep. Many patients also exhibit a postural tremor of the outstretched arms at a faster frequency of 6–8 Hz.

Rigidity

The patient complains of stiffness, pain or clumsiness in the affected limbs. On clinical testing of muscle tone, there is:

(a) lead-pipe rigidity (increased resistance to passive movement of the limbs throughout the range of movement that is equally present in flexors and extensors); or

(b) cogwheel rigidity (lead-pipe rigidity with superimposed tremor).

Rigidity in one limb can be made more apparent by simultaneously moving the opposite limb repeatedly (synkinesis). Rigidity can also be present in the trunk (axial rigidity).

Bradykinesia

There is slowness of initiation and execution of all movements as well as a general poverty of spontaneous movement. This may manifest itself in a number of ways:

(a) a mask-like expressionless face;

(b) reduced frequency of blinking;

(c) slurred, slow, low-pitched and monotonous speech that is without inflection;

(d) slow fine finger movements that are reduced in amplitude (tested by asking the patient to pretend to play a piano or to touch each finger in turn with the thumb of the same hand);

(e) micrographia (small and cramped handwriting);

(f) difficulty in changing positions (e.g. getting up from a chair or turning in bed); and

(g) a characteristic Parkinsonian gait (see page 66).

Posture and postural reflexes

Patients have a characteristic flexed posture, with the chin towards the chest, the back bent and the limbs flexed at the elbows and knees. As the disease progresses, the righting reflexes, which help to maintain posture, become affected and patients begin to exhibit postural instability. This can be demonstrated as a difficulty in maintaining posture when suddenly pushed forwards or backwards. Therefore, patients have a tendency to fall and, when they do, they are unable to stretch their arms to protect themselves.

Gait

In advanced disease, the patient may 'freeze' during walking and become rooted to the spot (see page 66).

Other features

• Cranial nerve findings

A number of ocular abnormalities occur. There is reduced frequency of blinking. Convergence and upward gaze may be limited, but voluntary horizontal saccades and pursuit eye movements are generally normal. There is a tendency to blink every time the direction of gaze is changed. Spasm of the orbicular muscle of the eyelids (blepharospasm) and flutter of the closed eyelids (blepharoclonus) are common.

The glabellar tap sign is elicited by repeatedly tapping the forehead. In normal subjects, this rapidly causes fatigue of the resulting blink reflex. In patients with Parkinson's disease, however, the blink reflex does not fatigue, although this is an unreliable sign.

• Limb findings

Power and reflexes are normal, as is sensory examination, even though patients often complain of painful legs.

• Autonomic features

The skin may have a greasy, seborrhoeic texture, and increased salivation and drooling of saliva are common. Constipation, urinary frequency, urgency and urge incontinence are also common, especially in men, who, in addition, often complain of impotence. Postural hypotension occurs, but to a much lesser degree than is found in multiple system atrophy.

• Psychiatric features

Although higher mental functions are preserved in the initial stages of Parkinson's disease, slowness of thought and memory retrieval (bradyphrenia) and changes in personality do occur as the disease progresses. Depression affects about 30% of patients and dementia eventually occurs in 15–20%. Acute confusional states also occur, but they are usually precipitated by drug therapy.

Course and prognosis

Parkinson's disease is a progressive disorder. Before the availability of drug treatments, the majority of patients were either severely disabled or dead within 10 years of onset. With modern treatments, life expectancy has improved greatly and now approaches that of a similar age-matched population.

Investigations

The diagnosis of Parkinson's disease is largely clinical, since conventional investigations, including brain imaging, are almost always normal. If the diagnosis is in doubt, a positive response to drug treatment is used as evidence in favour of idiopathic Parkinson's disease.

Management

Drug therapy

Drug therapy is aimed at correcting the dopamine–acetylcholine imbalance by enhancing the dopaminergic pathway or utilizing anticholinergic agents. There are six main groups of drugs in use:

• Levodopa

Levodopa (L-dopa) is a dopamine precursor that can cross the blood–brain barrier and therefore reach its site of action in the brain after oral administration. It is converted in the brain to dopamine. It is given in combination with a peripheral dopa decarboxylase inhibitor in order to prevent the peripheral metabolism of levodopa to dopamine, thereby enhancing the efficacy of levodopa and reducing the peripheral side effects (nausea, vomiting, hypotension). Two dopa decarboxylase inhibitors are available:

(a) carbidopa, which is combined with levodopa in Sinemet; and
(b) benserazide, which is combined with levodopa in Madopar.

Levodopa forms the mainstay of drug therapy for Parkinson's disease. It improves bradykinesia and rigidity to a greater extent than it does tremor. Treatment should be delayed until it is absolutely necessary, in order to prevent the adverse motor side effects. The dose of levodopa is gradually increased until either an adequate response is obtained or side effects limit further treatment ('start low, go slow').

Levodopa therapy benefits the majority of patients with Parkinson's disease. However, after about 5–10 years of therapy, most patients have a diminished response to treatment and have motor fluctuations and movement disorders. This is because:

(a)   the duration of action of the drug shortens, leading to a 'wearing off' effect;

(b)   unpredictable oscillations ('on–off syndrome') may occur, in which the patient switches from symptomatic benefit after taking the drug ('on') to an akinetic–rigid state ('off'), together with severe and often sudden episodes of immobility ('freezing'); and

(c)   dyskinesias and dystonic postures emerge; they may coincide with peak or trough drug levels or they may bear no relationship to the timing of the dose.

These late complications often respond partially to frequent, small doses of levodopa or controlled release preparations of levodopa. Alternatively, adjuvant therapy can be attempted.

• Dopamine receptor agonists
Dopamine receptor agonists directly stimulate the dopamine receptor. These agents act on dopamine D_2, D_3 and D_4 receptors but have variable effects on D_1 and D_5 receptors. The agents in clinical use are bromocriptine, pergolide, lysuride, ropinirole, cabergoline and apomorphine.

Other than apomorphine, these agents have an important role in early Parkinson's disease. They potentially delay the need for levodopa and thereby reduce the risk of the long-term complications. In addition to monotherapy, these agents are also used as adjuncts to levodopa.

Apomorphine is administered subcutaneously, as either an injection or an infusion. It is a useful agent in refractory, levodopa-related 'on–off' fluctuations.

• Anticholinergic agents
The anticholinergic agents include benzhexol, orphenadrine and benztropine. They are most effective in reducing tremor and have only a modest effect on bradykinesia and rigidity. They have a high incidence of side effects, which are attributable to peripheral cholinergic blockade (dry mouth, blurred vision, constipation and urinary retention) and central cholinergic blockade (memory and other cognitive impairment and confusional states); these side effects, especially the cognitive changes, limit their use in the elderly.

• Selegiline
The monoamine oxidase B inhibitor, selegiline, inhibits the breakdown of central

dopamine and thus allows greater availability of dopamine. It has a mild effect and is used in early Parkinson's disease (in order to delay the need for levodopa) or as an adjunct to levodopa.

• Entacapone

The catechol-O-methyltransferase antagonist, entacapone, like selegiline, inhibits the breakdown of central dopamine and thus allows greater dopamine availability. It too is beneficial as an adjunct to levodopa in patients who have a prominent end-of-dose wearing-off effect.

• Amantadine

Amantadine is an antiviral agent that has a mild beneficial effect in Parkinson's disease. Its modes of action include release of dopamine from the presynaptic terminals and inhibition of dopamine reuptake.

Surgery

Surgery is performed infrequently, being reserved mainly for severe cases and young patients.

• Stereotactic surgery

In stereotactic thalamotomy, a unilateral surgical lesion is made that diminishes contralateral tremor and rigidity but has no effect on bradykinesia. The procedure is associated with a 5–10% risk of stroke.

In stereotactic pallidotomy, a unilateral surgical lesion is made that diminishes contralateral levodopa-induced dyskinesia and has beneficial effects on tremor and rigidity.

Newer techniques involve surgical lesions to the subthalamic nucleus.

• Neurostimulation

More recent experimental techniques involve stimulation of the nuclei mentioned above rather than ablative techniques. This alternative has the benefit of having fewer permanent complications, such as stroke.

• Cell transplantation

Fetal substantia nigra transplantations into the striatum are viable and capable of producing clinical benefits. Investigations into their possible usefulness are currently ongoing.

Parkinson-plus syndromes

Multiple system atrophy

Multiple system atrophy describes three overlapping clinical entities that present in middle or late life.

• Striatonigral degeneration

There is degeneration of the substantia nigra and striatum but without Lewy bodies. The presentation is with parkinsonian features but usually without tremor, and the response to dopaminergic agents is poor.

• Olivopontocerebellar degeneration

There is degeneration of the olives, pons and cerebellum. The presentation is with cerebellar ataxia and the subsequent development of a variable akinetic–rigid syndrome. The Parkinsonian features show a poor response to dopaminergic agents.

• Shy–Drager syndrome

This syndrome is characterized by the progressive development of autonomic neuropathy in the form of:

(a) orthostatic hypotension;
(b) impaired gastrointestinal motility;
(c) sphincter disturbance causing urinary retention and incontinence;
(d) impotence; and
(e) loss of sweating.

Patients may show Parkinsonian features and cerebellar, corticospinal tract, cranial nerve and lower motor neurone dysfunction. The Parkinsonian features show an incomplete and short-lived response to dopaminergic drugs, which often exaggerate the orthostatic hypotension, thereby forcing their withdrawal.

Progressive supranuclear palsy (Steele–Richardson–Olszewski syndrome)

Progressive supranuclear palsy is a non-familial, progressive disease of middle and late life. It is associated with pathological features of neuronal loss, neurofibrillary tangles and gliosis in the basal ganglia and the upper brainstem. Its aetiology is unknown.

Clinically, it is characterized by akinesia, early loss of postural reflexes, falls, rigidity (which is predominantly axial), pseudobulbar palsy, mild dementia and supranuclear ophthalmoplegia. The supranuclear palsy initially affects down-gaze voluntary movements. Later, up-gaze and horizontal voluntary movements are also affected. However, a full range of eye movements can be produced by the 'dolls-head' manoeuvre, which evokes normal brainstem reflex eye movements.

The Parkinsonian features show a poor response to treatment with dopaminergic agents, and the median survival is about 6 years.

Corticobasal degeneration

Corticobasal degeneration is a progressive degenerative disorder of middle and late life. The pathological features include degeneration of the cerebral cortex (particularly the parietal and sensorimotor regions) and the basal ganglia.

The basal ganglia manifestations include Parkinsonian features (tremor, bradykinesia, rigidity and imbalance), limb dystonia and stimulus-sensitive myoclonus. Cerebral cortical manifestations include apraxia, cortical sensory loss and the alien limb phenomenon (wandering limb). Other features include athetosis, orolingual dyskinesia, disordered eye movements, dysarthria, dementia and upper motor neurone features in the limbs and the bulbar muscles.

There are no effective treatments.

Wilson's disease (hepatolenticular degeneration)

Wilson's disease is a systemic disease that ensues from abnormal copper metabolism.

Aetiology

Wilson's disease is inherited as an autosomal-recessive trait, the gene for which (on chromosone 13) codes for a copper-transporting ATPase.

Pathogenesis

The basic defect is a failure to excrete copper in bile, which results in copper deposition in various organs, particularly the liver and the brain. In addition, most patients also show a deficiency of caeruloplasmin, a copper-carrying glycoprotein.

Pathological changes in the liver vary from chronic active hepatitis to cirrhosis. In the brain, there is marked shrinkage of the basal ganglia; the cerebral cortex, brainstem nuclei and cerebellum are also involved.

Clinical features

The onset is usually in childhood or adolescence, with liver disease. Patients with liver disease may present with features of active hepatitis or chronic progressive cirrhosis with its associated complications. Sometimes, abnormal liver function tests are discovered incidentally. Patients with adult-onset, Wilson's disease, which is seldom later than 50 years of age, present with neurological and psychiatric features.

The neurological disturbance develops insidiously and presents as a variety of movement disorders, such as an akinetic–rigid syndrome, generalized dystonia or cerebellar ataxia. If the disease is left untreated, progression leads to dysarthria, dysphagia and muscular contractions owing to a combination of dystonia, bradykinesia and rigidity. Chorea, athetosis and seizures are uncommon, and sensory deficits or paralysis are not features of Wilson's disease.

The psychiatric manifestations include behavioural abnormalities, personality changes, affective disorders, psychoses and dementia.

Patients with cerebral dysfunction show copper deposition in Descemet's membrane of the cornea, giving rise to a pathognomonic sign, the Kayser–Fleischer ring.

Investigations

Serum copper is increased and caeruloplasmin is reduced. Urinary excretion of copper is increased. Liver biopsy shows an increased copper content in the liver tissue. MRI scans show evidence of brain atrophy with putaminal, thalamic or brainstem hypodensities.

Treatment

Chelating agents (D-penicillamine and trientine) promote excretion of copper from the body. Zinc is used to reduce the absorption of copper. Treatment halts and reverses both liver and brain damage, but the benefit may take months to appear. Treatment is for life and, without it, the condition is fatal within 5–15 years of onset.

Dyskinesias

Tremor

Tremor is an involuntary, rhythmic, oscillatory movement of one or more parts of the body. It is produced by either alternating or synchronous contractions of antagonistic muscles. The types of tremor are listed in *Table 5.2*, and the causes of tremor are listed in *Table 5.3*.

Resting tremor

This occurs in Parkinson's disease and other akinetic–rigid syndromes. (See Idiopathic Parkinson's disease, page 109).

Postural tremor

The causes of postural tremor are discussed below.

* Physiological tremor
This is a normal phenomenon that is present in all contracting muscle groups. It is a fine tremor that is barely visible to the naked eye; it is best observed by looking at the fingers of the outstretched hand. It is predominantly seen in the upper limbs, and its frequency ranges from 8 Hz to 13 Hz. A physiological tremor may be enhanced by various factors (see Table 5.3) and diminished by β-blockers.

* Essential tremor
Initially this tremor predominates in the upper limbs, but later the legs, head, face, vocal cords and tongue may also become involved. It has a frequency range of 4–8 Hz and it can be difficult to distinguish from an exaggerated physiological tremor. It may be familial, inherited in an autosomal-dominant manner, or sporadic. The tremor may temporarily improve with alcohol. Treatment is often not necessary, but if it is required, the tremor responds to β-blockers, benzodiazepines or barbiturates.

* Intention tremor
Causes of an intention tremor include cerebellar disease (see Co-ordination and cerebellar function, page 56) and rubral tremor.

Table 5.2
Types of tremor.

Resting tremor	Tremor that is present when the limb is relaxed and fully supported
Postural or action tremor	Tremor that is present during active maintenance of posture
Intention tremor	Tremor that worsens near completion of a movement
Task-specific tremor	Tremor that occurs only during a particular skilled movement (e.g. writing)

Table 5.3
Causes of tremor.

Resting tremor
Parkinson's disease
Other akinetic–rigid syndromes

Postural tremor
Physiological tremor
Exaggerated physiological tremor
   Anxiety states
   Endocrine disturbances—hyperthryoidism, phaeochromocytoma
   Drugs—sympathomimetics, antidepressants, lithium, sodium valproate
   Toxins—mercury
   Alcohol withdrawal
Essential tremor

Intention tremor
Cerebellar disease
Rubral tremor

- Rubral ('red nucleus') tremor

This is a coarse, severe, wide-amplitude tremor that affects the limbs, trunk and head. It often occurs with just slight movement. The cause is a mid-brain lesion affecting the dentorubrothalamic tract. It is called a rubral or 'red nucleus' tremor owing to the proximity of the lesion to this structure, although there is no evidence that this structure is involved in generating the tremor. Rubral tremor does not respond to either anticholinergic agents or β-blockers.

Chorea and athetosis

Chorea consists of a continuous flow of rapid, irregular, jerky and explosive movements that flit from one portion of the body to another in random sequence. It affects the face, trunk and limbs.

Athetosis consists of slow, writhing, purposeless movements that affect all muscle groups, particularly those of the face and upper limbs.

Chorea and athetosis often occur together—hence the term 'choreoathetosis'. Choreoathetosis arises from basal ganglia lesions (*Table 5.4*).

Huntington's disease

Epidemiology

Huntington's disease occurs worldwide in all ethnic groups with a prevalence of about 1 case per 20,000 people. The onset is usually between the ages of 30 and 50 years.

Table 5.4
Causes of choreoathetosis.

Drugs
    Neuroleptic drugs, antiparkinsonian drugs, oral contraceptives, phenytoin
Inherited disorders
    Huntington's disease
    Wilson's disease
Infections
    Sydenham's chorea (occurs in association with rheumatic fever)
Secondary to systemic disorders
    Immunological disorders
        Systemic lupus erythematosus, antiphospholipid antibody syndrome
    Endocrine disorders
        Thyrotoxicosis, hypo- and hyperparathyroidism
    Haematological disorders
        Polycythaemia rubra vera.
Vascular disorders
    Infarction, haemorrhage
Tumours
Trauma, including subdural haematoma

Aetiology

Huntington's disease is inherited in an autosomal-dominant pattern. The responsible gene is on chromosome 4 and is a trinucleotide repeat sequence. The gene normally codes for a protein, huntingtin, the function of which is unknown. The gene is fully penetrant, and thus the condition does not skip generations.

Pathology

The brain is generally atrophic with marked damage to the cerebral cortex, caudate nucleus and putamen. There is extensive loss of small neurones in these areas. These pathological changes result in marked reduction in acetylcholine and γ-aminobutyric acid.

Clinical features

Huntington's disease presents with psychiatric disorder or aberrant movements, or both. The psychiatric changes take the form of personality change, depression or, less frequently, psychosis. Later in the course of the disease a progressive dementia occurs. Initially, the movement abnormalities consist of clumsiness and twitching, but later a progressive generalized chorea emerges. Parkinsonian features, particularly bradykinesia and rigidity, and dystonia become increasingly prominent as the disease progresses. Some patients present with a Parkinsonian syndrome (the Westphal variant) instead of chorea.

Course and prognosis

Huntington's disease is a relentlessly progressive illness, with death occurring 12–15 years after onset.

Diagnosis

A positive family history clinches the diagnosis, but may not be readily available since it is often unknown or hidden. A genetic test is available for diagnosis.

Treatment

There is no cure for the condition, but neuroleptic agents or tetrabenazine may reduce the chorea.

Genetic counselling of all family members is essential. The genetic test can be offered to the relatives of sufferers, but this requires careful counselling since the disease develops later in life and is fatal. The test is also available for prenatal diagnosis.

Hemiballismus

Hemiballismus involves unilateral, sudden, violent, flinging movements that predominantly affect the proximal muscles of

Table 5.5
Causes of subthalamic nucleus lesions.

Infarction
Tumour
Trauma
Post-thalamotomy

the shoulder and pelvic girdles. It arises from a contralateral subthalamic nucleus lesion (*Table 5.5*). It usually remits over 3–6 months, but treatment with neuroleptic agents or tetrabenazine is often necessary because the movements exhaust the patient.

Dystonia

Dystonia is sustained muscular contraction that results in twisting and repetitive movements or abnormal postures. It is predominantly induced by action and it may improve with muscle relaxation or sleep. It occurs as a result of basal ganglia disorders.

Dystonia can be classified as being generalized or focal.

Generalized dystonia

In generalized dystonia, the abnormal movements occur in the muscles of the whole body. Some important causes of generalized dystonia are discussed below.

• Idiopathic torsion dystonia (dystonia musculorum deformans)
Most cases are inherited in an autosomal-dominant or autosomal-recessive pattern. The condition begins in childhood with an intermittent focal dystonia, usually affecting the lower limb. It gradually progresses to involve all the limbs, the trunk and the head over a period of 5–10 years. Medical treatment is often ineffective, but spontaneous remissions can occur.

• Dopa-responsive dystonia
This is inherited in an incompletely penetrant, autosomal-dominant pattern in association with mutations of a gene on chromosome 14. The gene product is involved in the dopamine synthesis pathway.

It begins in childhood or adolescence with dystonia of the lower limbs and the gait. The dystonia progressively worsens during the day and improves with sleep. Many patients develop Parkinsonism.

The response to small doses of levodopa, which bypasses the metabolic block and restores dopamine, is dramatic. Since the phenotype may be indistinguishable from idiopathic torsion dystonia, a trial of levodopa is essential in all cases of generalized or childhood-onset dystonia.

• Symptomatic dystonia
Dystonia can occur secondary to numerous diseases (*Table 5.6*).

Table 5.6
Causes of symptomatic dystonia.

Metabolic disorders
   Wilson disease, Niemann–Pick disease type C
Degenerative disorders
   Parkinson's disease, progressive supranuclear palsy, multiple system atrophy,
   Huntington's disease
Head trauma
Vascular disorders
   Infarction, haemorrhage, arteriovenous malformation
Tumour
Encephalitis
Toxins
   Manganese
Drugs
   Neuroleptics, dopamine agonists

• Paroxysmal dystonia

Paroxysmal dystonia is an inherited condition, usually an autosomal-dominant trait, in which brief episodes of dystonic posturing may follow sudden movement or noise.

Focal dystonia

In focal dystonia, the abnormal movements occur in the muscles of a single part of the body. Some important examples of focal dystonias are discussed below.

• Cervical dystonia

This is a sustained or episodic contraction of the neck muscles, which leads to lateral rotation (torticollis), extension (retrocollis) or flexion (antecollis) of the neck. It usually occurs in middle-aged or elderly patients and is usually a life-long illness.

• Blepharospasm and oromandibular dystonia (cranial dystonia)

Blepharospasm describes the recurrent involuntary spasms of eyelid muscles. Oromandibular dystonia describes the recurrent spasms of the muscles of the mouth, tongue and jaw. These conditions often coexist.

• Occupational dystonia

This dystonia affects certain repetitive activities that require good co-ordination. The best known example is dystonic writer's

Table 5.7
Causes of tics.

> *Simple tics—brief, repetitive, isolated movements (e.g. blinking)*
>   *Transient tics of childhood*
>   *Chronic simple tics*
> *Complex tics—repeated, sophisticated motor acts (e.g. touching the nose)*
>   *Gilles de la Tourette syndrome*
> *Symptomatic tics*
>   *Drug-induced tics*
>   *Post-traumatic tics*
>   *Neuroancanthocytosis*
>   *Focal brain lesions*

cramp, in which the patient typically develops a dystonic posture of the arm when gripping the pen.

Treatment

Focal dystonias show a variable response to anticholinergic agents. The treatment of choice is botulinum toxin injections into the affected muscles at about 3-monthly intervals.

Tics

Tics are brief, repetitive and stereotyped movements or utterances. They can be suppressed for variable periods of time, but only at the expense of mounting inner tension. The causes are listed in *Table 5.7*.

- Gilles de la Tourette syndrome

This is an inherited condition that shows autosomal-dominant traits with variable penetration.

It begins between the ages of 5 and 15 years with motor tics that affect the upper part of the body, particularly the face, neck and shoulders. Later, a constellation of motor and vocal tics, either simple or complex, develops. In about 60% of cases, the vocal tics become transformed into swear words (coprolalia). Tics alter with time and have a tendency for periodic remissions and exacerbations. They can be voluntarily suppressed for brief periods of time.

A significant proportion of patients also develop obsessive–compulsive disorder or attention deficit hyperactivity disorder, or both.

This is a lifelong disorder, although the severity diminishes with age.

Table 5.8
Causes of myoclonus.

Essential myoclonus—no known cause or neurological deficit
Myoclonic epilepsy—myoclonus with seizures dominating the clinical picture
Symptomatic myoclonus—myoclonus with encephalopathy
    Storage disorders
        Sialidosis, Gaucher's disease
    Degenerative disorders
        Huntington's disease, Parkinson's disease, progressive supranuclear palsy, multiple
           system atrophy
    Dementias
        Alzheimer's disease, Creutzfeldt–Jakob disease
    Infections
        Subacute sclerosing panencephalitis, herpes simplex encephalitis
    Vascular disorders
        Infarction
    Metabolic disorders
        Hepatic failure, renal failure
    Trauma
    Tumour
    Toxins
        Heavy metal exposure
    Drugs
        Levodopa, tricyclic antidepressants

Treatment of tics

Haloperidol, pimozide and fluphenazine are used to suppress tics. Clonidine may be beneficial both for tics and for attention deficit hyperactivity disorder, while fluoxetine may improve both tics and obsessive–compulsive disorder. The latter often needs psychiatric intervention.

Myoclonus

Myoclonus is a sudden, brief, shock-like, involuntary movement of part of the body or of the whole body.

Causes

Myoclonus can arise from dysfunction anywhere along the whole central nervous system. The differential diagnosis of myoclonus is broader than that of any other movement disorder, thus the list in *Table 5.8* is not comprehensive.

Drug-induced movement disorders

Many drugs can induce movement disorders (*Table 5.9*). In particular, dopamine receptor antagonists are associated with numerous movement disorders.

Acute dystonic reaction

Dystonia develops in 2–5% of patients within hours or days of commencing therapy with neuroleptics or antiemetics. The risk of this occurring increases with the size of the dose and is highest in young males.

The cranial, neck and axial muscles are commonly affected. The range of dystonic movements includes oculogyric crisis, grimacing, trismus (the jaw becoming fixed), torticollis, retrocollis and opisthotonus (the head and heels bend backwards and the body bows forward). These reactions are accompanied by considerable distress. If the offending drug is withdrawn but the dystonic reaction is left untreated, it can last for hours and recur for up to 2 days.

The reactions respond rapidly to the administration of intravenous anticholinergic drugs (e.g. benztropine and diphenhydramine). Intravenous diazepam may be effective as well. Oral anticholinergic therapy could be continued for 2–3 days to prevent recurrence.

Table 5.9
Examples of drugs that cause movement disorders.

Movement disorder	Drug
Postural tremor	Lithium, tricyclic antidepressants, bronchodilators, caffeine
Akathisia	Neuroleptics, dopamine depletors, SSRIs
Acute dystonia	Neuroleptics, metoclopramide, diazoxide, SSRIs
Tardive dyskinesia	Neuroleptics, antiemetics, levodopa, dopamine agonists, anticholinergics
Parkinsonism	Neuroleptics, dopamine-depleting agents, metoclopramide.
Neuroleptic malignant syndrome	Neuroleptics, metoclopramide, lithium, tricyclic antidepressants

Akathisia

Akathisia develops in 3–48% of patients over the first few weeks of treatment. It is both an inner sense of motor restlessness and motor manifestations resulting from attempts to satisfy the urge to move. It is a common movement disorder induced by dopamine antagonists. It usually develops within a few days of initiating drug therapy or increasing the dose (acute akathisia), although it can take months to appear (tardive akathisia).

Akathisia usually improves with drug withdrawal, but if drug treatment has to be continued it may respond to benzodiazepine or propranolol. Note that it does not usually respond to anticholinergic medications.

Drug-induced Parkinsonism

Approximately half of the patients who take neuroleptics on a chronic basis develop Parkinsonism. It usually develops gradually within the first month of treatment. The risk of developing Parkinsonism increases with the size of the dose and is highest in the elderly. Drug-induced Parkinsonism is clinically indistinguishable from Parkinson's disease, except that tremor is not a prominent feature.

The symptoms tend to recede gradually after several months despite continued neuroleptic therapy. Initially, the neuroleptic dose is altered or the offending drug is replaced with another agent that has less Parkinsonian effect. If Parkinsonism is still prominent, then an anticholinergic agent or amantadine can be initiated. Antiparkinsonian agents should be withdrawn after about 3 months in order as to assess the need for continuing treatment. Withdrawal of neuroleptic treatment eventually leads to complete resolution of symptoms.

Tardive dyskinesias

These are movement disorders that emerge in the setting of chronic neuroleptic treatment. The most common type is choreiform orolingual and masticatory movements (orofacial tardive dyskinesia), which consists of lip smacking and pursing, tongue protrusion, licking and chewing movements. Elderly patients are at a higher risk of developing choreiform dyskinesias, whereas all age groups are equally at risk of developing focal dystonia (tardive dystonia), which affects the cranial or neck muscles.

Approximately 60% of tardive dyskinesias will eventually improve if the causative agent is withdrawn, although initially this can cause a temporary exacerbation of the movement disorder. Orofacial dyskinesias may respond to treatment with tetrabenazine, reserpine or baclofen. Tardive dystonias may benefit from treatment with anticholinergic agents, reserpine or tetrabenazine.

Neuroleptic malignant syndrome

Neuroleptic malignant syndrome is characterized by generalized muscular rigidity, fever, an altered level of consciousness and autonomic disturbances such as tachycardia, hypertension or hypotension, urinary retention and sweating. Occasionally tremor, dystonia or chorea are prominent. Typically, creatinine kinase levels are markedly elevated.

Contrary to the impression given by the name of the syndrome, it can be caused by drugs other than neuroleptic agents. The syndrome can occur at any time during treatment, although it usually starts within a few days of initiating therapy, and it occurs more frequently with high potency and long-acting depot agents. Furthermore, an identical syndrome may develop after acute withdrawal of antiparkinsonian medications in Parkinson's disease.

Management consists of:

(a)   withdrawing the causative agent;
(b)   providing supportive care; and
(c)   treating with dantrolene or antiparkinsonian medications (levodopa and dopamine agonists).

Symptoms may persist for about 10 days after withdrawal of the causative agent, and even longer with depot agents. The syndrome is fatal in about 25% of untreated cases.

Epilepsy

6

Definitions

Epileptic seizures are intermittent, stereotyped disturbances of consciousness, motor, sensory, autonomic or psychic phenomena that ensue from abnormal repetitive discharges of cortical neurones. The pattern of clinical symptoms is determined by the origin of the discharge, its spread and its duration. Epilepsy is the recurring tendency to have such seizures. Clinically, epilepsy is defined as the occurrence of two or more unprovoked seizures.

Epidemiology

Epilepsy is a common neurological disorder with a prevalence of 0.5–1%. The lifetime prevalence of one or more epileptic seizures is 2–5%, and the incidence of new patients is 20–70 per 100,000 of the population per year; this is higher in childhood and adolescence.

Pathophysiology

Normally, the spread of electrical activity between neurones is restricted, and synchronous discharge of neurones involves only a small number of neurones. Such discharges are responsible for the normal rhythm seen on an electroencephalogram (EEG) recording.

During an epileptic seizure, large numbers of neurones discharge repetitively and synchronously owing to a failure of the inhibitory synaptic contacts between these neurones. This is seen on EEG recordings as high-voltage spike-and-wave activity.

Epileptic electrical activity falls into one of the following patterns:

(a) it may be confined to one area of the cortex (a 'partial seizure');

(b) it may start focally and spread to involve the whole cortex ('secondary generalization of a partial seizure'); or

(c) it may involve the whole cortex from the outset (a 'generalized seizure').

Any individual is capable of developing a seizure if exposed to a sufficiently severe metabolic or structural insult. Those who are more likely than others in the population to have seizures are thought to have a lower seizure threshold.

Aetiology

Aetiologically, epilepsy is classified into:

(a) idiopathic epilepsy (epilepsy of unknown cause or genetically determined epilepsy), which accounts for 60–70% of cases; and

Table 6.1
Factors that predispose to epilepsy.

Inheritance
Prenatal and perinatal factors
Trauma or surgery
Cerebrovascular disease
Tumour
Infections and inflammatory conditions
Metabolic disorders
Degenerative diseases
Drugs and toxins
Photosensitivity

(b) symptomatic epilepsy, in which the cause is known.

The common causes of symptomatic epilepsy are cerebrovascular disease (which accounts for 15% of cases), tumour (which accounts for 6%) and trauma (which accounts for 2%).

The factors that predispose to epilepsy are listed in *Table 6.1* and discussed below.

Inheritance

Genetic factors play an important role in the aetiology of epilepsy. A high degree of concordance is found in identical twins, and the incidence of epilepsy in near relatives of a patient is substantially higher than that in the general population. No single genetic trait can account for this highly heterogeneous condition. However, it is likely that genetic factors probably lead to alterations of cell membrane function or structure, thereby leading to a lowered seizure threshold.

Prenatal and perinatal factors

Intrauterine infections (e.g. rubella and toxoplasma), maternal drug abuse and fetal irradiation in early gestation can produce brain damage that may result in epilepsy. Perinatal trauma (causing cerebral contusion and haemorrhage) and fetal anoxia that is sufficiently severe to cause brain injury may also result in epilepsy.

Trauma and surgery

Severe head injuries are a potent cause of epilepsy. Post-traumatic epilepsy is described as:

(a) early post-traumatic epilepsy, in which the seizures start within 1 week of the injury; or

(b) late post-traumatic epilepsy, in which the seizures start after 1 week.

Post-traumatic epilepsy is most likely to occur when the injury is sufficient to cause coma. Early epilepsy increases in incidence with intracranial haemorrhage, whereas late epilepsy is more likely in the presence of a depressed skull fracture, cerebral contusion, dural tear, intracranial haemorrhage and early epilepsy.

Surgery to the cerebral hemispheres is followed by seizures in about 10% of patients.

Cerebrovascular disease

Seizures may follow cerebrovascular disease, especially in the elderly and in patients who have large areas of cerebral infarction or haemorrhage. Less common vascular causes of seizures include cortical vein thrombosis and arteritis (e.g. polyarteritis nodosa).

Tumour

Intracranial tumours, either primary cerebral tumours or metastases, can give rise to epilepsy, which is usually of the partial or secondary generalized type. The incidence of tumours as a cause of epilepsy increases with age of onset.

Infections and inflammatory conditions

Seizures may be the presenting feature or part of the course of meningitis, encephalitis or cerebral abscess. Seizures are also a manifestation of cerebral involvement in conditions such as systemic lupus erythematosus, sarcoidosis and Whipple's disease. It is of note that epilepsy is three times more common in patients with multiple sclerosis than it is in the general population.

High fevers caused by non-cerebral infections in children under 5 years of age can cause generalized seizures, which are also known as 'febrile convulsions'. These are usually self-limiting and, in most cases, there is no tendency for the seizures to recur in adult life.

Metabolic disorders

Disturbances of electrolyte homoeostasis can cause seizures. Examples include:

(a) hyponatraemia and hypernatraemia;
(b) hypoglycaemia and hyperglycaemia;
(c) hypocalcaemia;
(d) hypomagnesaemia;
(e) uraemia;
(f) hepatic failure;
(g) acute hypoxia; and
(h) porphyria.

Degenerative disorders

Patients with degenerative brain disorders have an increased risk of seizures.

Drugs and toxins

Many medications are associated with an increased risk of seizures, which can occur at both toxic and therapeutic concentrations. Examples of commonly used drugs associated with seizures are:

(a) phenothiazines;
(b) tricyclic antidepressants;
(c) selective serotonin-reuptake inhibitors;
(d) monoamine oxidase inhibitors;
(e) lignocaine; and
(f) theophylline.

Withdrawal of antiepileptic medications and benzodiazepines can also precipitate seizures.

Chronic alcohol abuse is a common cause of seizures. These seizures may occur while drinking, during abstention or as a result of hypoglycaemia. Illicit drugs, particularly cocaine, heroin, amphetamines and ecstasy also cause seizures.

Other toxic agents capable of causing seizures include carbon monoxide and heavy metals such as lead, mercury and tungsten.

Photosensitivity

Seizures are sometimes precipitated by flashing lights or flickering television screens.

Classification

No classification of epilepsy is entirely satisfactory because of the variety of clinical manifestations and causes. In 1981, the International Classification of Epileptic Seizures was proposed. This classification is descriptive and takes little account of the underlying pathology. *Table 6.2* summarizes the classification.

Clinical features

The diagnosis of epilepsy is essentially a clinical one; therefore, obtaining an accurate and detailed account of an attack is essential.

It is important to be familiar with the terminology used in describing an epileptic seizure (*Table 6.3*).

Some of the more common epileptic

Table 6.2
International Classification of Epileptic Seizures.

Generalized seizures
Absence seizures
   Simple (petit mal) or complex seizures
Tonic, clonic or tonic–clonic seizures
Atonic seizures
Myoclonic seizures

Partial seizures (focal or local seizures)
Simple partial seizures (consciousness preserved)—symptoms include motor, sensory, autonomic or psychic symptoms or a mixture of these
Complex partial seizures (consciousness impaired)—these begin as simple partial seizures and progress to impairment of consciousness, or there may be impairment of consciousness at the onset
Partial seizures evolving to secondarily generalized seizures

Unclassified

Table 6.3
Terminology used in the description of an epileptic seizure.

Prodrome or premonition
This is a vague sense that a seizure is imminent. This phase may last for hours or days

Aura
This is the subjective sensation or phenomenon that precedes and marks the onset of the epileptic seizure. It may localize the site of origin of the seizure in the brain

Ictus
This refers to the seizure itself

Postictal phase
This is the abnormal state of the patient in the time after the ictus until a full recovery

---

syndromes that are likely to be encountered in routine clinical practice are discussed below.

Generalized seizures

Primary generalized seizures appear to have a bilateral onset in the cerebral cortex. If a seizure begins locally and then evolves into a generalized seizure, it is called a secondary generalized seizure (*Fig. 6.1*).

Typical absence seizures (petit mal seizures)

Absence seizures occur in childhood and adolescence, and by adulthood they have usually disappeared or have been replaced by tonic–clonic seizures. The onset of absence attacks in adult life is rare.

Absence seizures occur without warning and consist of a sudden interruption of consciousness. The patient abruptly ceases whatever activity he or she is engaged in, as if frozen, and the eyes stare vacantly ahead. As a rule, the patient does not fall and occasionally even continues complex tasks such as walking. The attacks are sometimes associated with eye blinking and myoclonic jerks of the limbs or automatisms (performance of non-reflex motor activity during impaired consciousness, either during or after a seizure), in the form of lip smacking, chewing and fumbling movements of the fingers. The seizure usually lasts 2–15 seconds, at the end of which

normal behaviour resumes and the patient is often quite unaware of what has happened. The seizures frequently recur, sometimes up to several hundred times per day.

It is often possible to provoke an attack by asking the patient to hyperventilate for 1–2 minutes. Typical absence seizures are accompanied by a characteristic EEG abnormality of generalized spike-and-wave activity at a frequency of 3 Hz (see Investigations, page 70).

Tonic–clonic seizures (grand mal seizures)

In tonic–clonic seizures, loss of consciousness occurs, usually without warning, although in some patients there may be a variable prodrome and aura. The patient then enters the first phase known as the tonic phase.

The hallmark of the tonic phrase is that all the muscle groups contract strongly and the body becomes rigid, causing the patient to fall to the ground if unsupported. The eyes deviate upwards, the jaw muscles contract and the tongue may be bitten. Swallowing movements are lost and saliva dribbles from the mouth. Contraction of the chest muscles forces air out through the vocal cords in an involuntary grunt or cry, and respiratory movements cease, which leads to cyanosis. The elbows are flexed and the legs extended. Disordered contraction of abdominal and sphincter muscles may result in incontinence

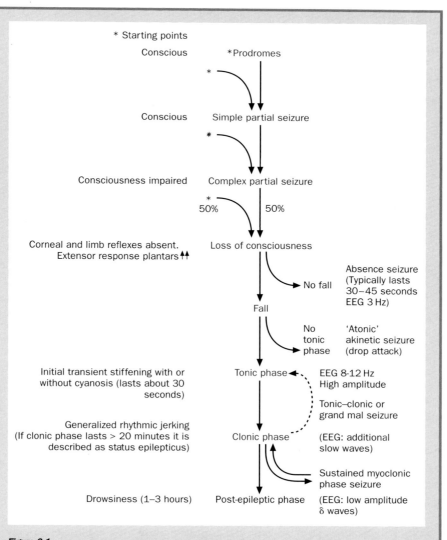

Figure 6.1
Sites of onset and features of different types of epileptic seizures.

of urine and faeces. The pupils dilate and are unreactive to light. This phase lasts for 10–60 seconds.

The tonic phase gives way to the clonic phase, in which the muscles jerk rhythmically. Autonomic signs are prominent and include tachycardia, hypertension, dilated pupils, salivation and sweating. This phase lasts for a few seconds to a few minutes, and the patient remains apnoeic until the end of this phase.

In the postictal phase, the patient is unresponsive for a variable period of time. This is followed by a period of drowsiness, confusion and disorientation.

Tonic or clonic seizures

Some patients experience only the tonic or the clonic phase of the sequence described above.

Atonic seizures

Atonic seizures are commonly called 'drop attacks' and are characterized by a brief loss of muscle tone. This loss of tone can be generalized and result in a fall, or it can be localized to muscles such as the nuchal muscles, resulting in head drop.

Myoclonic seizures

Myoclonus is a sudden, brief, shock-like, involuntary muscle contraction that arises because of central nervous system dysfunction. It produces a generalized or a focal jerk. It is a feature of many different forms of epilepsy.

Partial seizures

Simple partial seizures

A simple partial seizure arises in a localized area of the cerebral cortex, and there is no alteration of consciousness unless it evolves into a secondary generalized seizure. The clinical manifestations reflect the area of brain disturbance; most arise from foci in the sensorimotor cortex.

Simple motor seizures

Simple motor seizures arise in the motor cortex of the frontal lobe and cause jerking movements of the contralateral side of the face, limbs or trunk. Occasionally, spread of epileptic activity through the motor cortex results in a 'march' of the seizure from one muscle group to the next. This is known as a jacksonian march. After the seizure, the affected limbs may remain weak for some time, a phenomenon known as Todd's paresis.

If the supplementary motor cortex and the centre for voluntary gaze, which are situated in the frontal lobe anterior to the primary motor cortex, are involved, the seizure starts with the patient's eyes and head turning away from the lesion. These attacks are known as versive seizures.

Simple sensory seizures

Partial seizures that originate in the parietal cortex cause abnormal sensations in the contralateral part of the body. A sensory march can occur in much the same way as for simple motor seizures.

Other simple partial seizures

If the origin of the seizure is in the temporal lobe, a variety of interesting symptoms occur:

(a) olfactory or auditory hallucinations,
(b) emotional or psychic symptoms (e.g. *déjà vu*, which is a sensation that what is happening has already occurred at some previous time, or *jamais vu*, which is a perception that what is seen is so unreal that it bears no relation to previous life events);
(c) sensations of movements or rotation; or
(d) autonomic symptoms (e.g. palpitations).

Occipital lobe seizures are associated with visual hallucinations.

Complex partial seizures

A complex partial seizure arises from a localized area of the cerebral cortex and is accompanied by an impairment of consciousness. Complex partial seizures most often arise from foci in the temporal lobe; less commonly, they arise in the frontal lobe.

Temporal lobe seizures

A complex partial seizure may begin with impairment of consciousness or it may be preceded by the features of a simple partial seizure of the temporal lobe described above. Initially, the patient stares blankly and becomes unresponsive to questions or commands. However, certain complex acts, such as walking or even driving, may continue. The patient may develop automatisms such as lip smacking, chewing or swallowing movements, salivation, facial grimacing, hand gestures or aimless perambulation. Some patients may become violent and aggressive. Most complex partial seizures last for up to 2 minutes; postictally, the patient is amnesic for the period of the seizure, feels confused and sleepy, and complains of a headache.

Frontal lobe seizures

Complex partial seizures arising in the frontal lobes are often very similar to temporal lobe attacks, except that arm posturing, stereotyped movements of the legs and urinary incontinence are more common. In practice, it is often very difficult to distinguish between frontal lobe seizures and temporal lobe seizures.

Evaluation of seizures
History and physical examination

The diagnosis of epilepsy is primarily clinical, based on the description of the seizure. A

Table 6.4
The history and physical examination in the evaluation of seizures.

History
Detailed description of episode
    Obtain from patient and from witness
Past medical history
    Birth details
    Febrile convulsions in childhood
    Previous head injury
    Intracranial infection
    Tumour
Family history
    Epilepsy or neurological disease
Drug history
    Prescribed medications, recreational drugs, alcohol
Systems review
    Existing medical conditions

Physical examination
General examination
    Skin—neurocutaneous disorders (e.g. neurofibromatosis, tuberous sclerosis)
Cardiovascular system
    Pulse—arrhythmias
    Lying and standing blood pressure—postural hypotension
    Heart sounds—valvular disease
Abdomen
    Liver and spleen—alcohol, lymphoma, storage disorders
Neurological system
    Optic discs, visual fields, limbs (including power, reflexes, sensation)—intracerebral
        lesion
    A full neurological examination is essential to exclude any unsuspected pathology

detailed description of the episode needs to be obtained from the patient and from a witness. Examination during a seizure may reveal pupillary dilatation, tachycardia, hypertension, cyanosis and extensor plantar responses.

Investigations

A full discussion of the role of the EEG is given in Chapter 3, page 70. It is important to note that in the investigation of epilepsy the EEG is not always diagnostic.

Neuroimaging

CT or MRI scans of the head are usually recommended in the following cases of epilepsy:

(a) epilepsy of late onset;

(b) partial seizures;

(c) refractory seizures;

(d) epilepsy accompanied by abnormal clinical signs; and

(e) epilepsy that presents with status epilepticus.

In practice, adult patients who present with an isolated seizure will generally expect a CT head scan, despite the low yield and limited influence on management in such an unselected population.

Blood tests

Routine blood tests are used to exclude symptomatic causes of epilepsy. These tests are found to be normal in idiopathic epilepsy. During a generalized seizure the following abnormalities are found:

(a) arterial pO_2 and pH are lowered;

(b) serum creatine kinase is elevated; and

(c) serum prolactin is elevated.

These tests can be usefully employed to decide whether or not a seizure is epileptic in origin.

Differential diagnosis

It is important to distinguish epilepsy from other causes of loss of consciousness or transient focal dysfunction, since there are serious consequences when a diagnosis of epilepsy is made. *Table 6.5* provides a list of the differential diagnosis for epilepsy.

Pseudoseizures

Pseudoseizures are non-epileptic events that have a psychogenic origin and resemble

Table 6.5
Differential diagnosis for epilepsy.

Neurological disorders
Transient ischaemic attacks
Migraine
Vestibular disorders
Cataplexy and narcolepsy
Intermittent obstructive hydrocephalus
Cardiac disorders
Cardiac arrhythmias
Syncope
Metabolic disorders
Hypoglycaemia
Hyponatraemia
Hypocalcaemia
Dumping syndrome
Phaeochromocytoma
Renal failure
Hepatic failure
Psychiatric disorders
Pseudoseizures
Panic attacks

epileptic seizures. They can be extremely difficult to distinguish from true epileptic seizures, especially since they commonly occur in patients with epilepsy.

The following features are more likely to occur in psychogenic seizures than in epileptic seizures:

(a) gradual onset or progression of symptoms;
(b) bizarre and irregular movements; and
(c) behaviour influenced by the presence of an observer, by restraint or by suggestion during periods of apparent unresponsiveness.

An ictal EEG can usually distinguish between a psychogenic seizure and epileptic seizure; however, an abnormal interictal EEG does not rule out psychogenic seizures because psychogenic and epileptic seizures can coexist. Other features that can help to differentiate a pseudoseizure from an epileptic seizure are examination of the pupils, heart rate, blood pressure and plantar responses, and measurement of arterial blood gases and prolactin levels. If there is no evidence of epilepsy, anticonvulsants should be stopped.

Treatment
Pharmacotherapy
Initiation of treatment

Most clinicians do not start anticonvulsant therapy after the first seizure unless there is good historical or clinical evidence that further seizures are likely (e.g. a progressive cerebral disorder or a grossly abnormal EEG). When two or more unprovoked seizures have occurred, especially within a short period of time, anticonvulsant treatment should be considered.

Principles of treatment with anticonvulsant drugs

The therapeutic goal in epilepsy is to achieve freedom from seizures, although this is not always possible. If it is not possible, then reducing seizure severity becomes the objective. The likelihood of achieving this is greatly increased by adhering to the following principles:

(a) ensure good compliance through early and full discussion with both patients and relatives of the treatment options that are available and the possible side effects;
(b) use monotherapy whenever possible— epilepsy comes under control in 70–80% of cases using one drug alone, whereas

there is only a 10–15% chance of improving control by adding a second drug (but side effects caused by drug interactions increase significantly);

(c) start the drug at a low dose and increase the dose until seizure control is achieved or side effects from drug toxicity supervene—this ensures both that the lowest dose of the effective drug is used and that an adequate trial of a drug is performed before it is abandoned;

(d) measure anticonvulsant levels (except for sodium valproate)—it is important to note that the therapeutic range is a guideline and not an absolute, and that some patients achieve seizure control with blood levels below the reported therapeutic range while others tolerate blood levels well above this without any toxic side effects; blood levels are also useful for checking compliance;

(e) if an adequate trial of an appropriate drug fails to control seizures, consider the various possibilities:

(i) wrong diagnosis, particularly pseudoseizures (see above);

(ii) poor compliance, which can be revealed by blood anticonvulsant levels;

(iii) wrong drug (see (f) below); or

(iv) refractory epilepsy, which responds poorly to whatever medication is prescribed;

(f) if a drug fails to control seizures, introduce a new drug and increase the dose until seizure control is achieved or side effects from drug toxicity supervene; if the response is better, withdraw the first drug gradually.

Choice of anticonvulsant drug

The choice of anticonvulsant drug for a patient depends on its efficacy in the type of epilepsy that the patient has, the incidence and severity of side effects and its ease of use. *Table 6.6* gives the first-line anticonvulsants of choice for the different epilepsy syndromes.

The newer anticonvulsants (vigabatrin, gabapentin, topiramate, tiagabine) other than lamotrigine have an important role as adjunctive therapy, particularly for refractory partial seizures.

Table 6.7 summarizes the indications and important side effects of the anticonvulsant drugs.

The overall prognosis of epilepsy is good, and 75–80% of patients with generalized seizures can be maintained almost attack-free on monotherapy. The response of those with partial seizures, particularly complex partial seizures, is less predictable and often disappointing.

Discontinuation of therapy

The fact that anticonvulsant medications are associated with various side effects,

Table 6.6
First-line anticonvulsants of choice in various types of epilepsy.

Type of epilepsy	Recommended drugs
Partial seizures with or without secondary generalized seizures	Carbamazepine Sodium valproate Phenytoin Lamotrigine
Generalized tonic–clonic seizures	Sodium valproate Phenytoin Carbamazepine Lamotrigine
Absence seizures	Ethosuximide Sodium valproate Lamotrigine
Myoclonic seizures	Sodium valproate Clonazepam Ethosuximide Lamotrigine
Atypical absence, atonic and tonic seizures	Phenytoin Sodium valproate Lamotrigine Clonazepam Ethosuximide

teratogenicity and subtle effects on behaviour and cognitive function is an important argument for stopping treatment as soon as possible. Patients who have been in remission for 2–3 years should be considered for withdrawal of therapy. Against this is the risk of relapse.

The risk of relapse after anticonvulsant withdrawal in the first 2 years is 41% in adults and 30% in children, as opposed to 22% in patients continuing on medications. The risk of relapse is increased in adult-onset epilepsy, partial seizures, symptomatic epilepsy, epilepsy in which the EEG continues to be abnormal and epilepsy that was difficult to control before remission. An important consideration for withdrawal of therapy is the social consequence of a recurrence of seizures (e.g. driving prospects may be jeopardized).

The decision to withdraw therapy should

be taken by the patient in consultation with the clinician after weighing up all the benefits and risks. Withdrawal of anticonvulsants should be very gradual, over weeks or months.

Surgical treatment

About 15–20% of patients with epilepsy are refractory to anticonvulsant therapy. Some suitably selected patients may benefit from surgical intervention. The procedures available include:

(a) focal cortical resections, to which a patient with a well defined seizure focus is likely to respond well; it is most commonly used to excise small, focal temporal lobe lesions;

(b) hemispherectomy, which involves the resection of one cerebral hemisphere and is used in conditions in which the seizure focus is not localized but is limited to one hemisphere (e.g. unilateral congenital injuries); and

(c) corpus callosotomy, which is used to interrupt the pathways of spread of seizure activity rather than to excise or limit the seizure focus.

Social consequences of epilepsy

There is considerable social stigma attached to a diagnosis of epilepsy.

Employment

In certain areas of employment, there are statutory barriers to epileptic patients (e.g. the armed forces and many public services cannot recruit anyone with a history of seizures). Some occupations, such as those involving working at heights or with unguarded machinery, are clearly unsuitable. However, many employers are unwilling to employ patients with epilepsy, even in the absence of any statutory or safety barriers, simply because of discrimination.

Driving

Patients with epilepsy are barred from driving unless they satisfy the following conditions:

(a) they have been free from any epileptic seizures for 1 year; or

(b) they have had an epileptic seizure while asleep more than 3 years before the date when the license is granted and have had seizures only while asleep between the date of that attack and the date when the licence is granted; and

(c) driving is not likely to be a source of danger to the public.

More stringent restrictions apply to drivers of heavy goods vehicles and large passenger-carrying vehicles.

Clinicians should inform patients of these

Table 6.7
The indications and important side effects of anticonvulsant drugs.

Drug	Indication	Side effects	Comments
Carbamazepine	All forms of seizures except absence and myoclonic seizures	Rash, gastrointestinal upset, oedema, cognitive slowing, leucopenia, hepatotoxicity, bone marrow suppression	Absence of major effects on cognitive function is a major benefit
Clobazam	Refractory complex partial seizures Catamenial (menstrual) epilepsy	Sedation, dizziness, ataxia, headache, cognitive slowing	Value is limited by development of tolerance
Clonazepam	Refractory absence and myoclonic seizures	Sedation, dizziness, ataxia, muscle hypotonia, behavioural changes	Value is limited by development of tolerance
Ethosuximide	Simple absence seizures	Gastrointestinal upset, sedation, ataxia, headache, depression, psychosis, blood dyscrasias	Blood counts are required if there are symptoms or signs of infection since agranulocytosis or aplastic anaemia occur rarely
Gabapentin	Adjunctive treatment for refractory partial seizures	Sedation, dizziness, ataxia, headache, tremor, diplopia	
Lamotrigine	All forms of seizures	Rash, sedation, influenza-like symptoms, headache, diplopia	Can have a mood-enhancing effect
Phenobarbitone and primidone	All forms of seizures except absence seizures	Sedation, depression, ataxia, rash, confusion in the elderly and behavioural problems in children	Seldom used
Phenytoin	All forms of seizures except absence seizures	Sedation, dizziness, gastrointestinal upset, headache, insomnia, acne, hirsutism, coarse facies, rash, lymphadenopathy, neuropathy, blood dyscrasias particularly megaloblastic anaemia, hepatotoxicity, osteomalacia; ataxia, slurred speech, nystagmus and blurred vision are signs of overdose	There is a non-linear relationship between dose and blood level, which necessitates frequent blood-level monitoring

Table 6.7
Continued

Drug	Indication	Side effects	Comments
Sodium valproate	All forms of epilepsy	Weight gain, hair loss, gastrointestinal upset, tremor, sedation, thrombocytopenia, hepatotoxicity*	Monitoring blood levels is not useful (except to check compliance) since large variations throughout the day are common; blood counts and liver function tests before therapy and during first 6 months are required
Tiagabine	Adjunctive treatment for refractory partial seizures	Confusion, dizziness, gastrointestinal upset, fatigue, headache, tremor	
Topiramate	Adjunctive treatment for refractory partial seizures	Cognitive disturbance, ataxia, tremor, dizziness, gastrointestinal upset, weight loss, depression, renal stones (1–2%)	
Vigabatrin	Adjunctive treatment for refractory generalized tonic–clonic and partial seizures	Sedation, dizziness, weight gain, behavioural changes, depression, psychosis, visual field defects	Not recommended for use in patients with a history of mental illness

*Rare side effect.

regulations and advise them of their responsibility to inform the DVLA, which will make the appropriate decision. Patients should be advised to stop driving in the intervening period.

Leisure activities

Patients are encouraged to lead as unrestricted a life-style as possible but to take the necessary precautions (e.g. to swim only in the presence of a competent adult swimmer and to avoid activities such as boxing and rock climbing).

Epilepsy in women

Contraception

Women who take the oral contraceptive pill and are on enzyme-inducing anticonvulsants (e.g. phenytoin, carbamazepine, phenobarbitone or primidone) require a higher-dose oestrogen pill or a change to a different method of contraception.

Pregnancy

Ideally, patients with epilepsy on anticonvulsant treatment who wish to become pregnant should seek advice before conception. They require regular follow-up by their neurologist and their obstetrician. There are several specific considerations related to pregnancy as detailed below.

- Genetic aspects

A child has less than a 10% chance of developing epilepsy if one first-degree relative is affected, but this risk rises to 25% if two first-degree relatives are affected.

- Teratogenicity

The risk of epileptic mothers on anticonvulsant treatment having an abnormal fetus is about double that in normal women. All the first-line agents have some teratogenic effects on the fetus. The risk increases with therapy in the first trimester and polypharmacy. Thus, when a pregnancy is being planned drug withdrawal should be considered if there has been remission for 2 or more years, or polypharmacy should be reduced where possible. Generous folic acid supplements have some protective effects.

- Control of epilepsy during pregnancy

Epilepsy worsens during pregnancy in about 25% of patients, improves in about 25% and remains unchanged in the remainder. Various factors contribute to this including changes in the absorption, volume of distribution and metabolism of antiepileptic agents, and patient compliance. Close monitoring of blood anticonvulsant levels during pregnancy is therefore necessary to optimize control.

Breast feeding

There is insufficient secretion of anticonvulsant drugs in breast milk in the vast majority of patients to cause any symptoms in the infant.

Disorders of sleep and sexual function

Sleep

Normal sleep

Sleep is a recurrent, regular, reversible state that is characterized by quiescence and diminished responsiveness to external stimuli. In an awake subject the EEG is random and fast; however, when resting quietly, with the eyes closed, the EEG shows α-waves. Muscular tone as measured by electromyographic activity is high, and eye movements are present. The transition through drowsiness from being awake to sleeping is called the hypnagogic period, and during this time muscle tone diminishes, the eyes begin to roll and EEG α-wave activity decreases.

Sleep is divided into rapid eye movement (REM) and non-REM sleep. The normal pattern of sleep involves four or five cycles of alternating REM and non-REM sleep, with REM sleep becoming progressively more prominent as the period of sleep continues. The total time spent in REM sleep during an average night's sleep is 90 minutes, or 20% of the total sleep period. Other than brief periods of wakefulness (5% of the total sleep period) the remaining time during an average night's sleep (75%) is spent in non-REM sleep (*Table 7.1*).

Table 7.1
Stages of non-rapid eye movement (non-REM) sleep.

Stage 1 (5% of the total normal sleep period)
As the person falls asleep, α-wave activity diminishes to less than 50% of the EEG record, giving way to characteristic low-amplitude, low-voltage θ-wave activity. Occasional vertex sharp waves (V waves) are normal. Electromyographic activity decreases and rolling eye movements are present.

Stage 2 (55% of the total normal sleep period)
Now, in light sleep, the EEG shows low-voltage, low-frequency waves (θ-waves), which are interrupted intermittently by K-complexes and sleep spindles. K-complexes are high-voltage spikes consisting of a negative wave followed 0.75 seconds later by a positive wave. Sleep spindles are spindle-shaped EEG traces of short (0.5 seconds) bursts of waves (12–14 Hz).

Stage 3 (5% of the total normal sleep period)
The onset of deep sleep is accompanied by the appearance on the EEG of high-amplitude (75 μV), low-frequency (2 Hz) δ-waves, which, by definition, form less than 50% but more than 20% of the trace.

Stage 4 (10% of the total normal sleep period)
δ-Waves form more than 50% of the EEG activity. Collectively, stages 3 and 4 are called 'slow-wave sleep' or 'synchronized sleep'. Sleep spindles can occur in slow-wave sleep.

Table 7.2
Differences between rapid eye movement (REM) sleep and non-REM sleep.

	REM sleep	**Non-REM sleep**
Autonomic activity	Sympathetic	Parasympathetic
Heart rate	↑	↓
Blood pressure	↑	↓
Cerebral blood flow	↑	↓
Respiratory rate	↑	↓
Dreaming	↑	↓
Erection of the penis	Yes	—
Myoclonic jerks	Yes	—
Muscular tone	↓↓	↓
Ocular movements	Yes	Few

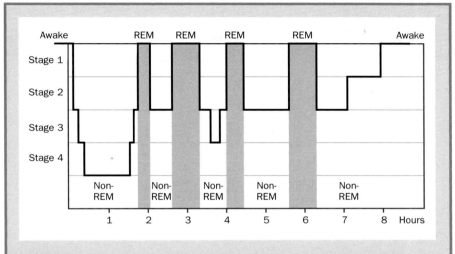

Figure 7.1
Hypnogram of typical sleep pattern showing rapid eye movement (REM) sleep, non-REM sleep and sleep stages 1–4.

REM sleep, also called paradoxical sleep, is characterized on the EEG by random, fast, mixed frequency activity of low-voltage with saw-tooth waves. REM and non-REM sleep differ in very many respects (*Table 7.2*).

Sleep can be plotted as a hypnogram (*Fig. 7.1*), and in a normal adult the pattern of sleep is as follows:

- after entering sleep, the person progresses through stages 1, 2, 3 and 4 and then returns to stage 3 and then stage 2;
- from stage 2, having been asleep for about 90 minutes, the person enters the first period of REM sleep;
- the person then reverts to stage 2 sleep and the cycle is repeated four or five times during the night with each cycle lasting 90 minutes;
- as sleep progresses the proportion of REM sleep increases and that of slow-wave sleep decreases.

The sleeping–waking cycle is thought to be governed by noradrenergic neuronal activity in the locus coeruleus and by serotonergic

Table 7.3
Sleep disorders.

Category	Type	Examples
Dyssomnias	Intrinsic	Hypersomnias
		Narcolepsy
		Restless legs syndrome
		Sleep apnoea syndrome
		Periodic limb movements
	Extrinsic	Environmental sleep disorder
		Inadequate sleep hygiene
		Substance-dependency
	Circadian	Jet lag
		Delayed sleep phase
		Shift work
Parasomnias	Arousal	Sleep-walking
		Sleep terrors
	Sleep–wake transition	Sleep-talking
		Rhythmic movement disorder
	Parasomnias with REM sleep	Sleep paralysis
		Nightmares
		Rapid eye movement sleep behaviour disorder
	Others	Enuresis
		Bruxism
Neurological and psychiatric disorders	Psychiatric disorders	Depression
		Psychoses
		Alcoholism
	Neurological disorders	Headaches
		Epilepsy
		Parkinson's disease
		Dementia

Table 7.4
Causes of insomnia.

Psychiatric causes	Depression, anxiety, mania, organic brain syndrome
Physical causes	Pain, arthritis, cardiorespiratory distress
Stressful life events	Bereavement
Physiological causes	Pregnancy, middle age
Environmental causes	Poor sleep hygiene, jet lag, shiftwork
Pharmacological causes	Alcohol, caffeine

neuronal activity in the raphe complex. However, as yet, the exact role of various 'sleep centres' and the neuronal mechanisms of sleep remain unclear.

Disorders of sleep

There are three main categories of sleep disorders (*Table 7.3*), and, despite their prevalence, they are afforded relatively little attention. Complaints about the quantity and quality of sleep are extremely common and are routinely dismissed by clinicians, largely because of poor understanding.

A detailed history is essential, noting the onset and duration of sleep, the presence and cause of any interruptions, the pattern of any daytime sleep and general sleep hygiene (bathing or eating before sleep, consumption of caffeine-containing beverages, exercising and the use of medications). In most cases this will provide a clear diagnosis. In a few instances a polysomnogram may assist in

making the diagnosis and guide pharmacological or surgical treatment; however, this is an expensive investigation that has limited use in many sleep disorders.

Insomnia

Insomnia, a non-specific symptom of many sleep disorders, is a common symptom that occurs in up to 40% of adults and perhaps an even higher percentage of the elderly. The many causes of insomnia are listed in *Table 7.4*. Of these, it is particularly important to exclude the psychiatric and neurological disorders. Many cases of insomnia can be helped by improving sleep hygiene.

Sexual function
Normal sexual function

Normal sexual function involves two major neurological pathways, both of which contain components belonging to the central and peripheral nervous systems and the autonomic nervous system. Impulses pass from the brain along the spinal cord and through a variety of nerves to genital blood vessels, muscles, skin and associated tissues. Sexual arousal and orgasm involve a complex series of events mediated by the autonomic nervous system. Genital stimulation is transmitted along the pudendal nerves to the spinal cord, from where some impulses continue to brain structures and others are relayed back to the genitalia via a spinal cord reflex. The structures involved are illustrated in *Fig. 7.2.*

Impairment of sexual function

Psychogenic sexual impairment is common, but neurological causes must be excluded. Indications of neurological sexual impairment include:

(a)   complete erectile dysfunction;
(b)   anorgasmia;
(c)   genital sensory loss; and
(d)   urinary incontinence.

Common neurological causes of sexual impairment include:

(a)   medication;
(b)   spinal cord injury;
(c)   diabetic neuropathy;
(d)   intervertebral disc herniation; and
(e)   multiple sclerosis.

It is therefore important to take a careful history and perform a thorough physical examination. Signs of particular significance are listed in *Table 7.5.*

Investigations can be carried out if there is still doubt as to the nature of the sexual impairment. Nocturnal penile tumescence is normal and occurs during REM sleep. This is an important test since nearly 50% of men with erectile dysfunction have an underlying illness. Those with psychogenic erectile dysfunction usually have normal nocturnal penile tumescence. Other tests that can be carried out examine the endocrine axes for abnormalities of hormone production and sensitivity.

Erectile dysfunction caused by neurological disorders can sometimes be treated pharmacologically or by means of mechanical aids and surgery. This usually necessitates specialist intervention.

Neurological disorders that can cause impairment of sexual function

Spinal cord damage

Spinal cord damage usually occurs because of an injury. The patient presents with weakness; quite often paraparesis with spasticity and brisk reflexes; sensory loss up to a specific level; and a combination of bowel, bladder and sexual problems.

Multiple sclerosis

Multiple sclerosis can present with sexual

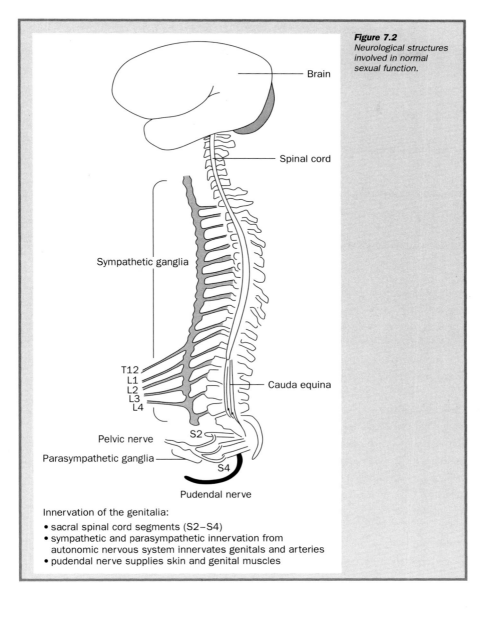

Figure 7.2
Neurological structures involved in normal sexual function.

Brain

Spinal cord

Sympathetic ganglia

T12
L1
L2
L3
L4

Cauda equina

Pelvic nerve

Parasympathetic ganglia

S2

S4

Pudendal nerve

Innervation of the genitalia:
- sacral spinal cord segments (S2–S4)
- sympathetic and parasympathetic innervation from autonomic nervous system innervates genitals and arteries
- pudendal nerve supplies skin and genital muscles

Table 7.5
Neurological signs of sexual impairment.

Site of injury	Signs
Spinal cord	Spasticity of the legs Urinary incontinence Paraparesis Sensory level
Peripheral nervous system	Loss of sensation in the saddle area Leg paresis and lack of reflexes Loss of scrotal, anal and cremasteric reflexes
Autonomic nervous system	Urinary incontinence Retrograde ejaculation Groin anhidrosis Orthostatic hypotension

impairment as the only complaint. However, more usually it causes erectile dysfunction, premature and retrograde ejaculation and anorgasmia. Multiple sclerosis is associated with poor sperm production but does not affect female fertility or pregnancy.

Diabetes mellitus

Almost half of diabetic men eventually develop some form of sexual impairment. It is not infrequently the first sign of diabetes and results from diabetic changes in genital arteries and damage to autonomic and peripheral nervous systems.

Medication

Almost all psychotropic medications interfere with sexual function, although it is

antihypertensive agents that are the most common cause of drug-induced sexual impairment. *Table 7.6* lists some of the more commonly used psychotropic medications that cause sexual dysfunction.

Table 7.6
Commonly used psychotropic medications that cause sexual dysfunction.

Antidepressants	Amitriptyline Imipramine Clomipramine Phenelzine SSRIs
Neuroleptics	Chlorpromazine Haloperidol Clozapine Risperidone

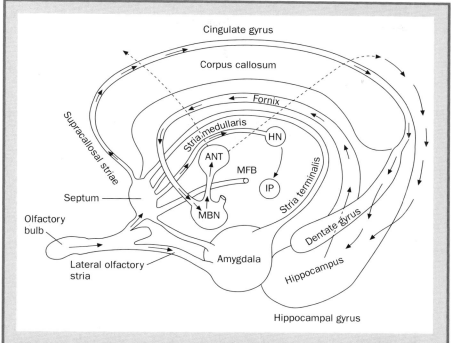

Figure 7.3
Components and connections of the limbic system. ANT, anterior nucleus of the thalamus; HN, habenular nucleus; IPN, interpeduncular nucleus; MBN, mammillary body nucleus; MFB, medial forebrain bundle. Adapted from Johnstone E, Freeman C, Zealley A, Companion to Psychiatric Studies, 6th edn. (Edinburgh: Churchill Livingstone, 1998).

Libido

Libido (sexual drive) is thought to originate in limbic structures (*Fig. 7.3*), and selective damage may lead to changes of sexual activity and interest. In most instances libido is diminished directly because of neurological damage or indirectly because of associated pain or sexual impairment.

Neurological disorders and depression

8

Depression

Clinical depression is a syndrome that consists of depressed mood, anhedonia and fatigue and that is present for a period of at least 2 weeks. It is a recurrent, often chronic illness that is associated with significant functional disability and an increased risk of suicide. It is a common illness that occurs more often in women than in men and that affects 3–5% of the general population at any one time. Many cases undoubtedly remain undetected, and, of those that are identified, many are misdiagnosed or inadequately treated.

The availability of a wide range of medications has made the management of depression more diverse and sophisticated. However, it is important to note that although many new antidepressant agents have been developed, there has not been so much of an advance in their efficacy as there has been in their side-effect profiles. For more than three decades, two main groups of antidepressants have featured in the treatment of depressive illness:

(a) tricyclic antidepressants; and
(b) monoamine oxidase inhibitors.

The development of selective reuptake inhibitors such as the selective serotonin reuptake inhibitors and the selective noradrenergic reuptake inhibitors grew out of a suggested need for greater selectivity. However, once again, compounds with actions on both noradrenergic and serotonergic systems (such as the dual-action antidepressant venlafaxine) are being favoured.

Monoamine theory of depression

The mechanisms involved in the monoamine theory of depression are shown in *Figs 8.1* and *8.2*.

The first tricyclic antidepressant to be discovered was imipramine, and the antidepressant effect of monoamine oxidase inhibition was first recognized with the antituberculous use of iproniazid. However, the monoamine oxidase inhibitors have never been used as widely as the tricyclic antidepressants, mainly because of their potentially dangerous side effects. At about the same time as the discovery of these antidepressants, it was noted that reserpine, an antihypertensive agent, caused symptoms of depression in some patients. Subsequent studies revealed that reserpine caused depletion of neuronal monoamine neurotransmitters (noradrenaline, dopamine and serotonin) and that this was probably responsible for its depressant action.

Conversely, tricyclic antidepressants and monoamine oxidase inhibitors enhanced monoamine neurotransmission by increasing the availability of neurotransmitters in the synapse. Imipramine was found to do this by inhibiting presynaptic neuronal reuptake of noradrenaline and serotonin, while the monoamine oxidase inhibitors achieved the same effect by inhibiting the degradation of neurotransmitter monoamines.

It was these observations that led to the monoamine theory of depression, which proposed that depression was a consequence of diminished monoaminergic neurotransmission caused either by a decrease in monoamines or by a reduction in receptor sensitivity at specific monoaminergic receptor sites. It is important to note, however, that the biochemical changes found in depression have not been explained by a single model or theory and that it is now thought that several neurotransmitter systems are likely to be involved in the pathogenesis of depressive illnesses.

Efficacy of antidepressant medication

Mild depression, as defined in the *International Classification of Diseases*, 10th edition, has been shown to benefit little from medication since it responds significantly to placebo and often remits spontaneously. Likewise, brief recurrent episodes of depression also show minimal improvement

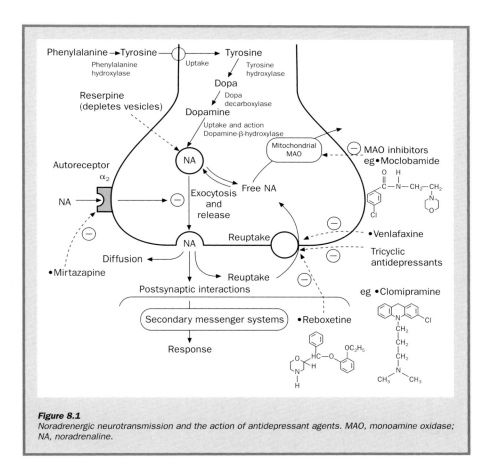

Figure 8.1
Noradrenergic neurotransmission and the action of antidepressant agents. MAO, monoamine oxidase; NA, noradrenaline.

with pharmacotherapy. However, more severe illnesses such as moderate depression and major (endogenous) depression show a much better response to pharmacotherapy, with more than two-thirds of patients eventually recovering.

A delay in the clinical response to antidepressant treatment of about 2–6 weeks with tricyclic antidepressants and selective serotonin reuptake inhibitors and a little longer with monoamine oxidase inhibitors is well recognized. The response to medication is

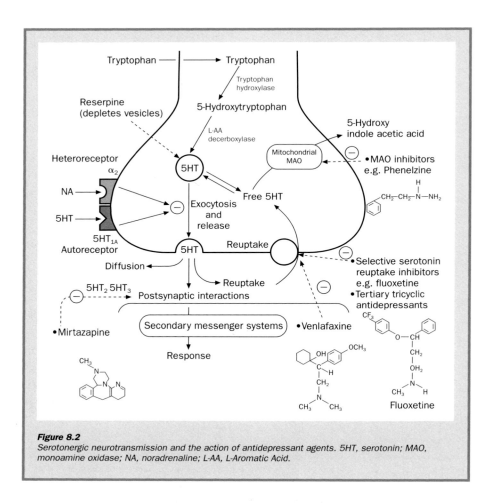

Figure 8.2
Serotonergic neurotransmission and the action of antidepressant agents. 5HT, serotonin; MAO, monoamine oxidase; NA, noradrenaline; L-AA, L-Aromatic Acid.

complex and variable, with some features of depression improving sooner than others. This makes it difficult to identify a specific point of recovery. The appropriate duration of treatment is a matter for clinical judgement,

although it should be noted that the presence of residual symptoms increases the likelihood of relapse, and so treatment should continue until the patient is symptom-free. Ideally, even after this stage, treatment should continue for a further 4–5 months since the premature withdrawal of medication may encourage relapse. The discontinuation of treatment should therefore be a timely, planned event and not one that is initiated by the patient because of intolerable side effects. Patients with multiple episodes and/or older age of onset may need to consider indefinite maintenance treatment.

Adverse effects of antidepressant medication

Traditionally, antidepressants have been classified according to their mechanism of action or chemical structure; therefore they either belong to one of the three main classes or have totally unique characteristics, in which case they are described as 'novel' or 'atypical'. Classification on the basis of similarities results in many shared adverse effects. Clinically, this is a matter of considerable significance because prescribing choice depends largely on the side-effect profile of antidepressants, which determines compliance, tolerance and risk in overdose.

Classes of antidepressant agents

Tricyclic antidepressants

Tricyclic antidepressants, so called because of their three-ring structure, are described as tertiary amines (with two methyl groups) or secondary amines (with one methyl group). Their therapeutic effects stem from their ability to block the reuptake of noradrenaline and serotonin. Secondary amines preferentially block the reuptake of noradrenaline, whereas tertiary amines mainly block the reuptake of serotonin.

However, they also act as antagonists at muscarinic, histaminic (H_1) and α-adrenergic receptors, producing predictable and well characterized side effects. The anticholinergic effects (dry mouth, constipation, blurred vision and urinary retention) of tricyclics are extremely common, although these are less severe with secondary amines. The side effects tend to diminish with continued treatment, but if they persist or are particularly troublesome they can be remedied with simple measures.

All of the tricyclics antidepressants with the exception of protriptyline and perhaps imipramine have a sedating effect, which may be of benefit to those suffering from insomnia. However, the sedating effect can be troublesome if it extends beyond sleep into the next day. The cardiovascular effects of tricyclic antidepressants include orthostatic hypotension and cardiac conduction abnormalities, and the postural changes in blood pressure can often cause dizziness and result in injury from falls. Tricyclic antidepressants also lower the seizure threshold and should therefore be used with caution in patients who suffer from epilepsy.

Furthermore, tricyclic antidepressants increase appetite, which leads to weight gain, and cause sexual dysfunction, a common and troublesome problem that is often overlooked. Most important, however, is the fact that the majority of tricyclic antidepressants are potentially fatal in overdose.

Monoamine oxidase inhibitors

Monoamine oxidase inhibitors are defined by their ability to inhibit monoamine oxidase. Moclobemide is a selective and reversible inhibitor of monoamine oxidase-A, whereas the remaining 'traditional' monoamine oxidase inhibitors (phenelzine, tranylcypromine and isocarboxazid) are irreversible and produce very different adverse effects.

Anticholinergic effects and hypotension are dose-dependent side effects of the traditional monoamine oxidase inhibitors, and although these effects are common, they may diminish or even disappear with time.

Like the tricyclic antidepressants, monoamine oxidase inhibitors can produce many forms of sexual dysfunction and commonly cause sedation and changes in weight. However, unlike the tricyclic antidepressants, they do not lower the seizure threshold and are less cardiotoxic.

The monoamine oxidase inhibitors are notorious for their many interactions with other medications and foods, which occur

through the inhibition of tyramine metabolism. However, moclobemide allows ingested tyramine to be metabolized and it is therefore much better tolerated. It also prolongs sleep without REM suppression, and it does not cause sexual dysfunction. Moreover, it too does not precipitate seizures or modify psychomotor performance and is therefore safe to use in epilepsy.

Selective serotonin reuptake inhibitors

Selective serotonin reuptake inhibitors have, as a group, steadily expanded, and there are now five agents: fluvoxamine, fluoxetine, paroxetine, sertraline and citalopram. Side effects are most prominent at the start of treatment. The side effects that are most commonly reported are nausea, insomnia and anxiety. Sexual dysfunction is also common and often leads to non-compliance; however, unlike the other groups of antidepressants, the selective serotonin reuptake inhibitors do not cause weight gain, and, overall, they have fewer side effects than the tricyclic antidepressants and the monoamine oxidase inhibitors.

However, their interactions with other drugs can have serious consequences because they inhibit a number of the hepatic cytochrome P_{450} enzymes, thereby increasing the blood levels of other drugs that these enzymes metabolize, such as the tricyclic antidepressants. When prescribed with monoamine oxidase inhibitors, the selective serotonin reuptake inhibitors can cause a serotonergic syndrome, in which there is a marked increase in blood pressure. Therefore, caution should be exercised when switching between different classes of antidepressants.

Novel antidepressants

Novel antidepressants cannot be placed in any of the above groups because of their unique pharmacology and mechanisms of action.

Mirtazapine

Mirtazapine is a dual-action antidepressant that enhances serotonergic and noradrenergic transmission and is an antagonist at $5HT_2$, $5HT_3$ histamine H_1 and presynaptic α_2-receptors. It lacks anticholinergic activity and is therefore better tolerated than the tricyclic antidepressants. It has a low propensity for drug–drug interactions since it neither inhibits nor induces hepatic enzymes.

Nefazodone

Nefazodone is a potent $5HT_2$, receptor antagonist. It inhibits both serotonin and noradrenaline reuptake and blocks α_1-adrenoceptors. However, it has relatively few side effects and rarely causes sexual dysfunction.

Reboxetine

Reboxetine is a selective noradrenaline reuptake inhibitor. By enhancing sympathetic function it can cause insomnia and anxiety, but it has little affinity for most other groups of receptors and consequently side effects are relatively uncommon.

Trazodone

Trazodone inhibits serotonin reuptake and is an antagonist at histaminergic and α_1-adrenoceptors. It is noted for its sedative effects, and it also commonly causes postural hypotension, dizziness, nausea and headache. However, it lacks anticholinergic effects and is less cardiotoxic than the tricyclic antidepressants.

Venlafaxine

Venlafaxine is a reuptake inhibitor of both noradrenaline and serotonin and at higher doses also dopamine. It is therefore a dual-action agent akin to many standard tricyclic antidepressants; however, it differs in that it has no cholinergic, histaminergic or α-adrenergic effects. It nevertheless does have some dose-dependent adverse effects. The most notable of these is nausea, which is usually short-lived. However, unlike most antidepressants, venlafaxine has few notable interactions and possesses a wide dosing range with corresponding gradation of efficacy, which make it suitable for the treatment of mild, moderate and resistant depression.

Neurological disorders and depression

There is considerable overlap of many psychiatric and neurological disorders. Depression is particularly important because it is common and carries a significant risk of suicide. However, detection, diagnosis and treatment can be difficult against the background of a neurological disorder, and, indeed, depression in these circumstances is often overlooked or thought to be 'understandable'.

It is difficult to estimate the prevalence of depression accurately since many depressive symptoms (e.g. anorexia, weight loss, poor sleep and fatigue) are also commonly found in neurological disorders. Furthermore, it is not always possible to distinguish neurological symptoms from somatization, and, consequently, the detection of depression is generally poor, with perhaps more than half of all of cases being missed. However, diagnosing depression solely on the basis of signs and symptoms, regardless of their source, could lead to overestimation. It is therefore important to note, first, that some depressive symptoms—guilt, worthlessness, hopelessness, unreactive mood and anhedonia—are less likely to arise solely as a consequence of physical illness and, secondly, that not all patients with neurological disease become depressed and that those that do can often be successfully treated.

The severity of a neurological disorder is naturally an important determinant as concerns the development of a depressive disorder; however, more significant are the disability and pain that it causes. Also important is the patient's ability to come to terms with the diagnosis and to cope with any associated disabilities.

Depression in the setting of a neurological disorder has several consequences. It is likely to worsen the prognosis and interfere with treatment by diminishing enthusiasm for treatment and compliance with it. Patients may have a reduced life expectancy and be less motivated and less likely to engage in therapeutic activities. Therefore, treatment of the depressive illness allows better management of the neurological disorder and improves the patient's quality of life.

When examining the mental state of a patient with a neurological disorder, there are some sensitive issues that need to be borne in mind.

A patient with a newly diagnosed neurological disorder may feel that questions concerning his or her mental state undermine the importance of the physical symptoms, and so it is appropriate to review these initially. However, the psychological implications should be carefully explored—in particular, the effect the disorder is having on day to day activities. The patient's understanding and knowledge of the illness should also be assessed, since the patient may be unaware of its true nature or may be in denial. Following this, the cognitive symptoms of depression should be sought and the risk of suicide carefully gauged.

If a depressive illness is discovered in the context of a neurological illness, then it should be treated promptly with due consideration of the various possible causes. The indications for the use of antidepressants are not especially different from those of depression generally, but the monoamine oxidase inhibitors should be avoided owing to their complex pharmacological interactions.

Psychological intervention has been shown to be effective in some cases, as long as the therapy is focused, initiated early and of relatively short duration. Most therapies aim to improve the patient's quality of life by educating the patient about the illness and helping the patient to adapt to the limitations and disabilities that it imposes. Cognitive behavioural therapy and problem solving are useful in these circumstances.

Epilepsy and depression

Epilepsy and depressive illness are associated in a number of ways. The diagnosis of epilepsy often leads to the development of depressive symptoms because of the nature of the illness and its social stigma. Depressive symptoms can occur in the prodrome, be an ictal phenomenon or manifest after the seizure as postictal depression. Postictal depression is often severe and difficult to manage, having much in common with psychotic depression. Depressive episodes between seizures are relatively common and this interictal depression is often variable in its intensity and duration, with abrupt, unexpected onset and remission.

The risk of suicide in an epileptic patient is increased five-fold in comparison to that in the general population, and it is a further five-fold higher in temporal lobe epilepsy. The risk of deliberate self-harm is also greater in patients with epilepsy, and so the development of depression is a serious concern.

The treatment of depression in an epileptic patient involves balancing the risk of precipitating seizures against the need to treat the depressive illness with physical measures, namely antidepressants and electroconvulsive therapy. All antidepressants are likely to increase the risk of seizures, either directly via effects on receptors and membranes, or through pharmacokinetic interactions with anticonvulsants. Tricyclic antidepressants tend to increase the occurrence of seizures because of their effect of lowering the seizure threshold, whereas monoamine oxidase inhibitors (especially moclobemide) and selective serotonin reuptake inhibitors carry relatively little risk of inducing seizures. Clinically, the risk of an antidepressant-associated seizure can be minimized by monitoring and maintaining therapeutic blood levels of anticonvulsant medication.

In some patients with epilepsy and depression, electroconvulsive therapy may be necessary. Psychological treatments should be considered in all such patients and particularly in patients who have considerable difficulty in adjusting to the illness. Depressive illness in the setting of epilepsy should be treated as necessary, accepting the fact that there may be a period during which the epilepsy is less well controlled.

Further Reading

Clinical neurology textbooks

Bahra, Cikurel. *Crash Course. Neurology.* (London: Mosby, 1999)

Ginsberg L. *Lecture Notes on Neurology*, 7th edn. (Oxford: Blackwell Science, 1999)

Perkin GD. Mosby's color atlas and text of neurology. (London: Mosby-Wolfe, 1998)

Clinical neurology reference books

Adams RD, Victor M, Ropper AH. *Principles of Neurology*, 6th edn. (New York: McGraw Hill, 1997)

Marsden CD, Fowler TJ. Clinical neurology. (London: Arnold Publishers, 1998)

Bradley WG, Daroff RB, Fenichel GM, Marsden CD. *Neurology in clinical practice.* (Boston: Butterworth-Heinemann, 1991)

Neurology examination textbooks

Fuller G. *Neurological examination made easy.* (Edinburgh: Churchill Livingston, 1996)

Medical Research Council. *Aids to the examination of the peripheral nervous system.* (Eastbourne: Balliere Tindall, 1986)

Depression and epilepsy books

Malhi GS, Bridges PK. *Management of Depression.* (London: Martin Dunitz, 1998)

Betts T. Epilepsy. *Psychiatry and Learning Difficulty.* (London: Martin Dunitz, 1998)

Index

Page numbers for figures and tables are in **bold**.